D0592082

30 Ways Managers Shoot Themselves in the Foot

(And How to Avoid Them)

Bill Lee

New Oxford Publishing Corporation

This publication is designed to provide accurate and authoritative information in regard to the subject mattered covered. It is sold with the understanding that neither the publisher nor the author are engaged in rendering legal or accounting advice. If legal or accounting advice is required, the services of a competent attorney or CPA should be sought.

Editor: Hilary Kanter
Cover design: Foster & Foster
Interior design and composition: Greenleaf Book Group LP

Published by New Oxford Publishing Corporation

This book is available at special quantity discounts to use as premiums and sales promotions, or for use in corporate training programs. For more information, please call the Special Sales Manager at 800-476-8722, ext. 42369, or write to New Oxford Publishing of North America, P.O. Box 5558, Greenville, SC 29606.

Library of Congress Control Number: 2005933600

ISBN 10: 0-9723165-1-5
ISBN 13: 978-0-9723165-1-4

Printed in the United States of America

10 9 8 7 6 5 4 3 2

To my father, Clarence G. Lee, whose confidence in me survived many tests. It was his entrepreneurial spirit and the example he set that gave me the courage to leave the security of a corporate job and start my own business in 1987. God bless his memory.

Contents

Foreword

I was born into a family business.

In 1894, my grandfather, William Franklin Lee, and his two brothers, Robert Malcolm Lee and Jessie Thomas Lee, founded Lee Hardware Company in Dallas, Georgia, a small town 32 miles northwest of Atlanta. All three men possessed an entrepreneurial spirit. In an era when virtually everyone in their rural county was a farmer, the Lee brothers abandoned the profession they were born into and founded a family business.

My grandfather was extremely frugal. To save scarce cash to provide for his wife and eight children, he walked a half-mile to work each day, carrying his lunch in a small black lunch pail. My grandparents grew most of their food and raised livestock for meat and eggs, so the basic needs for survival were always met.

As the business began to prosper, my Uncle Bob and my Uncle Jessie invested the dividends they received from the business into farmland and into rental property, while my grandfather reinvested in the business. This practice enabled him to eventually own a majority of the outstanding shares.

A few years after the business was founded, disaster struck. The business was destroyed by fire. There was no insurance in those days, but the Lee brothers had earned a strong reputation in the community and among their suppliers as hard-working men who knew how to manage a business and earn a profit. But most importantly, they had earned a reputation as men of their word.

Following the fire, Beck & Gregg Hardware Co., their Atlanta-based hardware wholesaler, replenished their inventory on the strength of a handshake. They rebuilt the store, replaced the inventory, and were soon back in business.

Like me, my father, Clarence Gordon Lee, spent much of his youth hanging out at the family hardware store. Born in 1907, my father was injured in a freak accident at the age of 16, lost a year of high school, and made the decision to abandon the idea of graduating. He joined the family business as a full-time employee in 1923. There were few titles in those days; each member of the Lee family spent most of each day waiting on trade, putting up and organizing stock, sweeping and cleaning the store, and interacting with customers. There were no income tax laws in those days, so administrative duties were less intensive, certainly less than they are today.

Store hours were from 6 a.m. until 6 p.m. except for Saturdays, when the business was open until 9 p.m. On Saturdays, many of the county folk would come into Dallas, the county seat of Paulding County, to purchase their provisions for the coming week. Lee Hardware was a popular place for many of the store's customers to loiter. Perhaps one reason the store was so popular was because when televisions first came to our community in the mid-1940s, the store had two or three on display. Lee Hardware Company was the place many residents of Paulding County saw their first television program.

I was born in 1941. As a child, hanging out at the hardware store was one of my most enjoyable pastimes. Summertime was especially fun. I recall cutting open fresh watermelons brought to the store as gifts from farmers who were both good customers and good friends. We would eat the watermelon in the back of the main store building, and from a rear door that was propped open on hot days, toss the rinds out onto the back street for passing cars to decimate.

In the fall and winter months, I remember parching peanuts on the stove in the back of the store. Each morning, tradesmen would arrive at the store shortly after it opened, stand around a propane gas stove in the back, drink coffee, eat freshly parched peanuts, and visit until the tradesmen, one by one, would decide it was time to go to work.

Tom Carruth was a plumber. Sometimes Tom was on the store's payroll, but other times he was an independent contractor who depended on Lee Hardware to sell his services and handle his paperwork.

Tom's brother, John, not only waited on "trade" at the store, he also took over from my father driving the company's newest and largest truck to Atlanta each week to pick up material from our wholesale suppliers. John began taking me along as his "helper" when I was six years old. Over the ensuing 10 years, I learned to drive and became familiar enough with the streets of Atlanta that my father allowed me to drive the truck to Atlanta the first summer following my 16th birthday, a thrill that has rarely been exceeded as my career developed and took a different direction.

"Bully" Wills was another long-time employee. His son, Kenneth Wills, was also a full-time employee at Lee Hardware. He and Tom Carruth fought on the front lines in World War II. As a kid, I loved to ride along with my dad on the half-mile drive to the store and listen to their war stories until it was time for me to begin my half-mile walk from the store to school.

Opal Graham was my dad's right-hand person. She not only kept the books, she also had tremendous product knowledge, so she could wait on customers with great confidence. Opal and her husband, Ray, were active members of our church and remain close family friends to this day. Opal and another friend, Judy Hardy, were as dedicated to my mother after my dad passed away in 1976 as any family member could possibly have been.

Homer Freeman was a painter who would use no other paint than the Glidden brand our store sold. He was a great guy who loved wrestling. I'll never forget when one of our local "boys," Bob Shipp, who had become a professional wrestler, came to Dallas to compete in the town's first professional wrestling match. It was held at the local high school gymnasium, and my dad invited his good customer—and personal friend—Homer to attend the match. I was invited to come along.

I particularly remember an occasion when Shipp's opponent tied him up in the ropes and proceeded to beat him half to death—well, that's what it seemed like to me—and Homer jumped up from his ringside seat to help Shipp free himself from the ropes.

Homer's youngest son, Billy, was a high school buddy of mine. He worked at Lee Hardware for several years and is now part owner of a local hardware store.

Customer service was in the Lee brothers' blood. It was never the topic of conversation. No seminars were ever attended. No customer service books were on the office shelves. It just seemed to be the logical way to do business. My dad, the non-relatives who worked in the store, and the other Lee family members were extremely close to their customers.

We always knew when someone knocked on our front door that it was a stranger; neighbors and friends always came around to the back door. During my childhood there were dozens of nights when a customer—someone my dad may or may not have known well—knocked on the front door and asked my dad to drive into town and open up the store for a small item that was somehow essential to either their home or business.

A lot of folks in our county owned chicken houses, so on really cold nights, if a valve broke in the gas heating system, the chickens would instinctively pile on top of each other to keep warm. So if the valve wasn't replaced quickly the chickens would smother, and the farmer's livelihood would be lost.

Another vivid memory is how my dad, other family members, and employees at the store would wrap a purchase before accepting payment. A large roll of brown paper was positioned in a rack on the counter along with a cone-shaped roll of white twine. My dad was masterful at effortlessly wrapping items such as a toaster, electric razor, or a radio. When he finished wrapping the item, he would present the wrapped package to the customer as if it contained a fine piece of jewelry.

It was the Lee family's policy to discuss family business issues in private. As a child, neither my cousins nor I were ever privileged to know what went on in family meetings. In all towns, but especially in small towns, gossip spreads pretty quickly, so the Lee family made sure that neither spouses nor their children would be in a position to talk out of school.

I do remember that each year at the family reunion—usually held at my Lee grandparents' home—my father and his seven siblings would disappear to participate in a private family conference to discuss any issues that needed all family members present to resolve. The spouses and the children went about their business of visiting and playing, oblivious to what may have been going on behind closed doors.

In one of those family meetings, my father, who was the managing partner, told his siblings that he wanted to purchase their shares. This was not a demand, but a request. He told his brothers and sisters that he could not achieve his personal financial goals unless he could increase his percentage of ownership in the business. I was not privileged to know which sibling said what, but I do know that they all ultimately agreed to sell my dad their shares, which gave him the same majority ownership that my grandfather had owned prior to his death.

Following World War II, my dad made the decision to add building materials to the company's product offering. He received considerable criticism from the older partners for purchasing lumber, roofing, gypsum wallboard, and so on, in carload quantities. But they trusted his business judgment and, although sometimes reluctant, gave him their support. Adding building materials enabled Lee Hardware Company to more than quadruple its sales in less than five years.

Introduction

When I graduated from Emory University in Atlanta in 1963, I made the decision not to join the family business, but rather pursue a different direction for my career. With a degree in psychology, I worked for a short time in the psychiatric ward at Emory University Hospital, but soon moved from a clinical environment into corporate America. My first job was with the Atlanta Newspapers, where I earned $100 per week. After 12 months on the job, I received only a $5 per week raise—which incidentally was double the raise my colleagues received. This was my first experience in corporate America, but I was bright enough to realize that such a modest raise in pay would not get me to where I wanted to be financially. After all, my boss earned only $120 per week; his boss earned $140; his boss earned only $160; and the director of the entire division earned only $20,000 per year. I decided to look around to see what else might be available for a young man with a degree in psychology and a willingness to work hard.

About this time, my dad introduced me to a salesman who represented the old Ruberoid Company, an asphalt roofing manufacturer. In 1967, Ruberoid was acquired by GAF Corporation. The salesman's name was Marion Talley. In his college days, Marion had been an all-American football player at Auburn University. He was also a referee in the Southeastern Conference; my dad had pointed him out to me when we would watch bowl games on TV during the Christmas holidays.

One day when I was visiting my dad, Marion happened to be making a sales call. He told me about a job
opportunity on the Atlanta sales team. The job paid $200
a week—which definitely got my attention—and I could
continue to live in Atlanta. So Marion set up an interview for me with his sales manager. While the salary
and commission was projected to be double my current
level of income, I really didn't want to be a salesperson.
I was pretty naïve in those days and wanted to do something for a living that I considered to be important, and
I didn't consider selling roofing to be very important, so
I turned the job down.

My wife thought I was nuts, as did my dad. But Marion
Talley didn't give up on me. He called a good friend of
his who was sales manager in Mobile, Ala., a man by the
name of Doc Knudsen. Marion explained that he knew
a young man in Atlanta who he believed had a talent for
sales but who also had a distorted view of the sales profession. He asked Doc if he would give me a call and see
if he could sell me on coming to work for GAF.

Knudsen called and offered to pay to fly me down
to Mobile for an interview. I still didn't want to be a
salesperson, but I had never flown on a jet airplane, so
I accepted the invitation just because I wanted to fly on
a jet.

When I arrived in Mobile, Knudsen picked me up
at the airport and took me out to dinner. He asked me
dozens of questions about where I wanted to go in my
career, how much money I envisioned earning down the
road, what I objected to about the profession of sales,
and so on. To make a long story short, Knudsen sold
me on leaving Atlanta and moving to Mobile for a job

in sales, traveling lower Alabama and southern Mississippi as far as the Louisiana state line. The job paid a monthly salary of $400 plus commission. I earned just shy of $11,000 in my first year.

In 1967, Knudsen recommended me for a senior sales territory in Tidewater, Virginia. Living in Virginia Beach, I worked for Karl Miller, sales manager in GAF's Baltimore district. In this territory, I earned just over $18,000 in commission income. Then in 1968, my fondest dream came true—I was offered a promotion to sales manager at GAF's Savannah plant. Even though this management job paid significantly less—$15,000 annually—I was a manager, a goal I had set for myself when I first interviewed with Doc Knudsen in 1965.

I left Virginia Beach for Savannah in a driving snowstorm. I was on Cloud Nine. I couldn't believe it, I was going to be a manager. I couldn't wait to begin pulling the strings, calling the shots, making decisions, and doing all the things I envisioned managers did. I could see myself jetting up to our New York City headquarters to sit in on strategic planning sessions and participating in high-level corporate meetings. I couldn't wait to begin hiring new sales talent, training salespeople, and showing the company what I could accomplish as a manager.

When I arrived in Savannah for my first day on the job, my boss showed me a map of our district, gave me a list of the salespeople who would be reporting to me—well, they really reported to both of us [see Management Mistake #7]—and told me to select a salesperson from the list, give him a call, and schedule to ride with him on some of his sales calls. I was given no goals, no objectives, no training, no management training, no do's and don'ts—nothing, nada, zilch.

In the 12 months I spent as a sales manager, I believe I made every mistake in the book. All I learned was how much I didn't know about management.

During the year prior to my arrival, the Savannah district had lost a million-dollar customer when that customer was acquired by a large national chain that bought a competitive brand of roofing products. So I was assigned the personal responsibility to nurture a start-up company that top management believed could replace the million dollars of sales volume we had lost, and then some. The company was South Carolina-based Builder Marts of America, Inc. (BMA). BMA was an unusual sort of company. It was a buying group, but not a nonprofit cooperative like all of the other buying groups in the U.S.; BMA was owned not by its dealer customers, but by its management team.

When I attended BMA's annual dealer meeting during the winter of 1968, Clarence Bauknight, the company's CEO, told me that if I would ever consider changing jobs, he would like to talk to me about becoming a part-owner in BMA. I thanked him politely, but made no commitment at that time. But the more I thought about it (that is, the idea of part-ownership, being based in South Carolina near enough to my hometown for my children to visit their grandparents and not having to face the possibility of relocating every few years), the more the idea appealed to me.

On a business trip from Nashville to Asheville, N.C., to Savannah, I called Clarence and asked if I could stop by for a visit. Bauknight and I made a deal on the spot.

Although I would earn a salary of only $13,500, I was given a bonus opportunity and, most important, an opportunity to buy BMA stock. I had no money to use for the stock purchase, but BMA arranged with a local bank to accept the stock as full collateral. Now I was not only a manager, but also a part-owner. Life was good.

It was during my 19-year career at BMA that I really learned how to manage. Clarence Bauknight, Tom Mills, Wade Stephens, and other senior managers literally taught me everything I was to know about management. We grew BMA from a start-up in the late 1960s to a $640 million company by 1986, my last full year at BMA.

In 1987, I sold my interest in BMA and formed Lee Resources, Inc., a consulting, training, and publishing firm. At Lee Resources, we have conducted more than 1,000 consulting assignments and seminar programs. The recommendations I make in the following chapters to help managers avoid shooting themselves in the foot come from the management techniques I learned at BMA and from the mistakes I have observed in my 18-year consulting practice.

MANAGEMENT MISTAKE

1

Failure to Hold Managers Accountable for Measurable Results

In the hundreds of management seminars I've conducted over the course of my career, I have always told my audiences that if I ever were to write a book about management, the first chapter would be on the importance of being able to pinpoint responsibility. I believe it's extremely important to the success of an organization for managers to be able to point their finger at each person in the organization and hold each employee accountable for measurable results.

To me, this is a basic rule that will enhance the odds that a business will achieve its long-term goals. Without measurable goals to keep the organization focused, there's a strong tendency for the people who make up the organization to become more task-focused than goal-directed. Hard work is certainly important, but not unless the hard work leads to desired results.

No one should make the mistake of believing they are measured by how tired they are at the end of the day. Fatigue is not the objective; the objective is results achieved, regardless of how hard managers and employees work.

In many companies with whom I have consulted, employees are hesitant to take action before touching base with a supervisor. As a result, employees—many of whom are managers themselves—are not growing and developing in management confidence as they might if they knew how their jobs were being measured and had the authority to make the decisions necessary to achieve these measured goals.

Without clear-cut accountability, employees are not at all sure what they have to do to get ahead in the organization. When this is the case, the result is too much pressure on the owners or on top management, since those at the top are the only ones who do know what's expected of them in measurable terms. Too often, it's only top management that suffers when the company falls short of established business goals.

All employees need to know how they are measured to achieve an optimal level of effectiveness. In the absence of this knowledge, it is difficult for employees to know what they have to do to gain management's favorable attention.

On consulting assignments, I often ask managers and other key employees, "How is your job measured?"

In response, the person might ask, "How do you mean, exactly?"

"Well, another way of phrasing the question might be to ask, what do you have to do to get feathers in your cap? You know, what would you have to do to get a pat on the back from your boss?"

An all-too-common answer to this question is, "The managers at this company don't hand out feathers."

Other times I hear, "When the boss is not yelling at me, I know that I'm doing okay."

In the Position Specifications we prepare *(see Chapter 4)* when my company sells a recruiting assignment, we always include how the job will be measured. Most candidates would think it's unreasonable to accept a position unless they understood in very specific and measurable terms what they have to do to be successful.

CEOs or general managers might be measured on their ability to achieve a specified pretax profit margin, return on assets, return on stockholders' equity, or compounded growth objective.

Credit managers might be measured on their ability to achieve an agreed-to number of average collection days and hold bad expense to a specified percentage of sales.

Buyers might be measured on how well they do at turning inventory, minimizing back orders, or on the gross margin their product group achieves.

Salespeople might be measured on how well their actual sales compare to their sales budget, the dollars of new business they are able to attract to the company, and their overall gross profit margin.

A manufacturing supervisor might be measured on how many units are produced over a specified time frame, perhaps how well the organization performs against quality standards, or how well the manufacturing unit performs against cost guidelines.

A factory worker might be measured by personal output, safety, quality, attendance record, and so on.

Delivery drivers might be measured by how many stops they make in a day, their safety record, the accuracy of their work, the number of compliments and complaints they receive, etc.

An expression we consultants and trainers like to use with our clients is, "Your raise becomes effective when you do." In other words, if you want to get a raise, you have to meet or exceed your measurable goals.

ACTION STEP: Beside the names of each of your employees, jot down what you want each of them to do more of and what you want each of them to do less of. This will give you a good start at identifying measurable accountability for each of your people.

ACTION STEP: Make a list of each job function in your organization and list the criteria you will use to measure the performance of each of the job holders.

ACTION STEP: Make sure that each person on your business team is given the authority to make the decisions necessary to succeed. A bad decision is not indicative of a bad manager; managers learn by trying new techniques and feeling the freedom to make mistakes as long as they learn from them.

MANAGEMENT MISTAKE 2

Failure to Set Short-term Goals for the Business

If you don't know where you're going, any road will take you there. This is an old saying that is doubly true in business—especially in a family business where multiple family members frequently hold leadership positions.

Many decisions that are made over the course of the year have a longer-term effect on the business than merely solving the issue at hand at that particular moment in the life of the business. So if owners and managers wish to gain optimal traction with each decision they make, they should put their heads together and determine both the long- and short-term goals for the business.

One of the best examples of a short-term business goal is the annual budget. *(See Chapter Three.)* The annual budget—or profit plan, as I frequently call it—includes goals for sales, gross margin, operating expenses as a percentage of sales, inventory, accounts receivable, capital expenditures, and so on.

Just as there is a current portion of the company's financial liabilities (that portion that must be satisfied within the next 12 months), there are current portions to long-term planning; that is, the portion of the long-term plan that will be implemented over the coming 12 months.

In addition to the annual budget, the following are some of the questions that should be answered as a result of the company's short-term planning process:

1. What capital expenditures will be necessary this year?
2. What repairs, additions, or expansions will take place this year with regard to the company's physical facilities?
3. What new product lines do we plan to add?
4. What changes, if any, will we make to our accounts receivable policy this year?
5. What changes, if any, will we make to our employee policy manual (benefits, holidays, sick leave, etc.) this year?
6. What staff positions do we anticipate adding during the coming year?
7. What staff positions will be eliminated during the coming year?
8. What new systems and procedures will we add or eliminate?
9. Will we add a new location this year?

Even if these questions are answered with "no change," it is wise to at least take a fresh look at each of these questions—and others—every year in order to decide if changes in the local, state, national, or industry climate call for different answers.

MANAGEMENT MISTAKE

Failure to
Pay Yourself First

Many times when businesses don't earn an optimal level of profitability, it's because management failed to prepare a plan for producing a satisfactory bottom line.

A profit plan is a projection of how much the business is going to sell, how much gross margin it is going to achieve, how much it is going to spend, and how much it is going to earn on the bottom line during the coming year. It's as simple as that. In fact, preparing a profit plan is one of the easiest ways to just about guarantee that the company will improve its bottom-line performance.

I will be the first to admit that in my family, my wife and I don't budget our household income and expenses. I have been blessed in many ways throughout my business and personal life, and one of them is with respect to our income. We have always been disciplined enough to live beneath our means; that is, spend less than we earn.

However, if my family were to experience financial problems, if we were to find ourselves accumulating credit card debt because we were living beyond our means, the first thing we would do would be sit down together and prepare a household budget.

First, we would project our income for the coming year.

Then we would budget our household expenses and control them—by category—to make dead sure that we have our spending under control to the point that we could pay off our debts and get our financial lives in order.

By category, I'm referring to major categories of expenses such as groceries, eating out at restaurants, entertainment, house payment or rent, clothing, dry cleaning, utilities, vacation, car payment, capital expenditures for home repairs, automobile repair, insurance, etc.

Most businesses, quite frankly, are simply processing too many financial transactions for managers to keep up with them all by the seat of their pants; that is, by keeping an eye on the balance in the company's checkbook. They need a profit plan to ensure that when the end of the year rolls around, they're putting optimal dollars on the bottom line.

I read a terrific book a few years ago that supports the profit-planning concept. The title of the book is "The Richest Man in Babylon" (see Appendix II). The author, George S. Clason, tells of a wise old man who taught a younger, not-as-wise man the secret to financial success. One of the rules he espoused in the book was to "pay yourself first."

Let me paraphrase a few of the lessons this little book offers for managing the financial aspects of a business:

"But isn't everything I generate in my business mine?" the young man asked his mentor.

"That's your problem," the wise old man answered, "you're paying everyone else but yourself. You're paying your vendors, your employees, the utility companies, your insurance agent, the tax collector. What you're failing to do is to pay yourself. This is why your bottom line is so anemic."

Based on this principle, we recommend the following profit-planning process to our clients:

1. How Much Money Do You Plan to Put on the Bottom Line Over the Course of the Next 12 Months?

Based on return on sales, return on investment, return on assets, industry standards (how you arrive at your organization's profit goal is your choice), determine how much you believe your company should earn on the bottom line before income taxes to achieve an optimal level of performance. To determine this number, take a look at some industry statistics to determine what average and optimal earnings you should strive for. If you belong to an industry association or if there are consulting firms that target your industry, both would be a great place to begin your research.

Another technique is to take a look at your earnings over the last couple of years and try to improve upon those numbers.

2. How Much Do You Plan to Sell?

Don't just pull a number out of the air; do some research! For example, interview each of your salespeople and a few of your key customers. In doing your homework, try to figure out what economic conditions are projected for your trade area during the coming year.

There are only three basic ways to raise sales:

1. Sell more to current customers.
2. Attract new customers to your company.
3. Introduce new products that you have not offered for sale in the past.

Will you be adding a new location during the coming year? Will you be adding any new products that you've not sold before? Looking into these areas should give you enough information to make an informed sales projection for the coming year.

3. How Much Do You Plan to Spend Next Year?

Begin with your personnel-related expenses, since the people portion of your total expenses will most likely make up the lion's share of total operating expenses.

Begin by listing all employees down the left-hand side of an electronic spreadsheet or an accounting pad. In the column to the right of the employees' names, list their current hourly (if applicable) income or monthly salary. In the next column, list their total compensation for the current year.

In the fourth column, jot down the pay raise you plan to give each employee, based on that person's performance. In the fifth column, jot down how much the raise represents as a percentage increase. In the sixth column, jot down how much you project the employee will earn during the coming year.

The percentages of each increase will come in handy as you compare the raises you're giving each employee and as you attempt to keep pay raises in line with the sales increase you project over the previous year.

If you project that you'll be hiring new staff during the coming year, obviously you won't yet know their names, so designate the new hires by placing an "x" under each category (salespeople, warehouse personnel, drivers, administrative, manufacturing personnel, and so on).

In the appropriate column following each "x" and under the month you believe you will actually bring the new employee on board, project both the hourly, monthly, and ultimately the annual wage you believe you will need to pay each new hire. This will enable you to take not only existing employees into consideration, but new hires, as well.

EXCESSIVE COMPENSATION: If you are the owner of a privately held business, you are permitted to pay yourself whatever you believe you can afford. However, when you do choose to pay yourself a salary that is substantially higher than industry averages for your position in the company, you may have to make some adjustments in your profit plan.

I recommend that owners do enough research to determine how much they would have to pay a world-class manager if they were to have a recruiter find such a manager for them. In fact, an industry recruiter is a good place to begin your research. Your state or regional trade association executive is another excellent source of this kind of information.

For example, let's assume that the *going rate* for a top-notch general manager is $100,000 per year, but the owner wants to pay himself or herself $150,000. This decision is one that I call the "privilege of ownership." But to maintain the integrity of the profit plan and to allow owners to pay themselves whatever they wish, I recommend that beside the owner's name in the budget, jot down a salary of $100,000. Then create a new line on the income statement (P&L) that reads "Before Taxes and Bonuses."

Below that line, insert the owner's name and the $50,000 in additional income he or she plans to take out of the business.

Following the personnel-related (salaries, group medical, workers' compensation, payroll taxes) section of your profit plan—based on what you spent last year and taking into consideration how much you plan to increase sales—estimate how much you will spend on expense categories such as insurance, property taxes, postage, repairs and maintenance, training, dues and subscriptions, business travel, repairs and maintenance, etc. Many of these expenses will increase in direct proportion to the amount of the sales increase, but others will increase at a rate that is completely independent of sales. For example, if OPEC cuts oil production, gas and oil prices will most likely rise whether or not your company's sales increase.

4. Back Into Gross Margin

At this point, you know how much you plan to earn, how much you plan to sell, and how much you plan to spend. So if these projections are reasonably accurate, how much does your gross margin have to be in order to make the plan come true? Unlike your other projections, you must back into your gross margin projection for the coming year.

Let's say that your gross margin over the past three years has averaged 27.4%, and when you back into the gross margin you must have to make your plan come true, that "plugged" number comes in at 28.1%. If this were the case, I'd say that it is reasonable to expect to achieve your objectives.

On the other hand, if when you back into your gross margin you need to earn more than 31% to make the plan come true, your profit plan is perhaps unrealistic. So you can raise sales, figure out how to increase gross margin or lower expenses as a percentage of sales, but the bottom-line number that was arrived at by making reasonable projections must remain almost sacred.

Reduce your bottom-line objective only as a last resort, or you will be hard pressed to ever achieve optimal earnings.

Rome was not built in a day, and neither is a highly profitable company. It takes time to turn a marginally profitable company into an organization that has earnings in the upper quartile of your industry. So be patient, but also be realistic.

5. Capital Expenditures

The annual profit plan should also include a budget for capital expenditures. Capital expenditures differ from operating expenses in that they are primarily balance sheet items, although additional operating expenses can sometimes be required as a result of the capital expenditure. For example, a new delivery vehicle might require hiring a new driver, or a new piece of manufacturing equipment might require hiring an additional employee to operate it. The capital expenditure budget will help management predict how much capital they will need to borrow or otherwise generate during the coming year.

6. Manage "By the Numbers"

Once you've completed the profit plan, run the business "by the numbers."

Management should think twice before allowing operating expenses as a *percentage of sales* to exceed budget. Any time you violate your budget, you're "betting on the come." In other words, by intentionally committing more dollars to operating expenses than your budget calls for, you are gambling that sales will increase sufficiently to prevent these higher-expense dollars from exceeding your budget as a *percentage of sales*.

The key to managing a business by the numbers is to keep operating expenses as a *percentage of sales* in line with the budget, not necessarily in line with budgeted expense *dollars*.

Making the decision to invest more dollars in operating expenses than the profit plan calls for is an important management decision. Management must decide whether the best course of action is to exercise self-discipline and wait until sales can justify the additional expense dollars, or take a calculated risk and bet that the additional investment will generate the additional sales necessary to keep the profit plan intact.

A typical scenario occurs when the sales force tells management they could improve sales if management would invest in a new $100,000 delivery vehicle, which would also require that the company hire an additional driver.

My recommendation for management is to take a page out of my negotiating seminar and ask the sales force this question: "*If* we come up with the capital for the new truck and *if* we exceed our budget for truck drivers, what dollar amount of additional sales volume will you commit to?"

NEGOTIATING RULE: *NEVER* give up anything unless you at least attempt to get something in return.

Businesses that take the time to prepare a well-designed profit plan and manage the business by the numbers will almost always earn more money on the pretax line than businesses that run the business by the seat of their pants.

MANAGEMENT MISTAKE

Failure to Establish
Hiring Guidelines

When a business is in the market for a computer system, decision makers assess the company's needs and prepare a list of specifications to help them make the best possible decision. The same is true regarding a new office copier or a new telephone system. Just any computer system, copier, or telephone system won't do; when you make an investment of this size, you want to make sure that the product you purchase meets the criteria established in the list of specifications.

While any intelligent manager would give considerable time and attention to these kinds of capital purchases, it is amazing how many of these same managers will make hiring decisions based on gut feel or intuition that will end up costing the company a lot of money.

How much does it cost your company when you make a bad hiring decision? It can cost a lot—often many thousands of dollars. And when you consider lost opportunities, disappointed customers, or the poor decisions a bad hire can potentially influence, the cost can run up into the stratosphere.

To reduce the odds of making a bad hiring decision, I recommend that my clients take the time to thoroughly analyze each position in their company and prepare a position specification for each. The position spec is not unlike the specifications you would prepare for a major purchase, it's just that you are investing in a person instead of a piece of equipment.

There are several common mistakes managers make that can be significantly reduced by going through the position-specification process:

Mistake #1: Hiring the Best of the Bunch

This mistake most often occurs when managers become frustrated with their efforts to find the right person for the job. So in their desperation, they say to themselves—and sometimes to others in the organization—"I'm getting pretty tired of all of the inconvenience we're going through from being shorthanded on our sales counter. I'm going to hire somebody by the end of the week even if I'm not convinced that the person is right for the job. Maybe we can spend a little extra time developing a training program to get them up to speed."

That kind of statement is the kiss of death. When managers are guilty of hiring the "best of the bunch," odds are excellent that they will soon have to go through the entire hiring process all over again when the "best of the bunch" candidate doesn't work out.

RULE: When the first *bunch* of candidates doesn't produce a person who meets your position spec, get yourself a new bunch to choose from. Hold out until you find a candidate who meets the specifications you specified for the position.

Mistake #2: Wishful Thinking

This hiring mistake occurs when managers hire a candidate they know does not possess the "right stuff" for the job, but they convince themselves that with an intensive training program and a lot of hand-holding, the person will grow into the job, developing the ideal behavior that he or she doesn't currently possess.

This is a cop-out. While candidates who don't possess the behavioral profile the job calls for might very well grow and develop, the odds are quite low, however, that an adult will make these kinds of life-changing adjustments to their innate abilities.

Mistake #3: Stop Selling Until You're Ready to Buy

During an interview with a candidate, how much of the talking is being done by you? Until I was trained in the art of interviewing, I'll bet I spent more than 75% of my interviewing time selling the candidate on the benefits they would receive if they came to work for our company, leaving less than 25% of the interview time to determine if the candidates met the criteria I had established for the job.

Remember this! You learn nothing when you're doing the talking. You learn only when you're *listening*.

So stop talking so much and begin asking well-designed, open-ended questions that provide solid evidence of the candidate's qualifications for the specific job you have in mind.

For more information on how to design interview questions, see Appendix III.

The Position Specification

To begin the process, you and other key people in your organization should spend the time necessary to answer some questions about the person you hope to recruit for the job.

At Lee Resources, we have designed questionnaires to assist managers in this process. (*See Appendix IV.*)

Most of the questions are generic, so they can be used for multiple positions in the company, but you might want to design a few that are specific to a particular job.

Key Questions

QUESTION #1: Is it possible that there is someone currently on the payroll who qualifies for the position, or at least should be seriously considered?

While most managers may have already considered this possibility, it is important to systematically review a list of current employees to determine if the open position is an opportunity for advancement or well-suited for someone already on your business team.

QUESTION #2: What are a few of the characteristics of the previous jobholder that you will miss most?

This question is designed to make managers focus on the positive behavioral characteristics of the individual being replaced that they would like to duplicate in the successful candidate.

QUESTION #3: What are some characteristics of the previous jobholder that management would most like to avoid in the successful candidate for hire?

This question is the exact opposite of Question #2 and is obviously designed to force management to concentrate on the negative characteristics possessed by the previous jobholder that they wish *not* to duplicate in the successful candidate.

QUESTION #4: Is it possible that the position could be eliminated?

Although this is a long shot, I believe it's wise to always ask yourself this question. Occasionally, I find that a position can be eliminated by dividing the duties of the position among others in the organization.

Once the manager or members of the hiring team have completed the questionnaire, the company—after carefully analyzing their answers to each question—is in a position to begin writing the position specification.

When selecting each word, sentence, and paragraph on the position specification, keep in mind that the finished document will ultimately become one of management's most valuable **marketing tools** as it searches for Mr. or Ms. Perfect. There will be more on the use of the position spec as a marketing tool later in this book.

The position spec is made up of four parts:

1. A brief overview of the job and compensation plan.
2. Who the position reports to.
3. How the successful candidate's performance will be measured.
4. The behavioral requirements of the job.

See Appendix I for a sample of a completed position specification.

Psychological Testing

Well-designed psychological tests are reliable tools to assist managers in determining an individual's psychological makeup, including personality characteristics, values, and talents each candidate uses in the decision-making process.

In the testing division and the recruiting division at Lee Resources, we use a series of three psychological instruments, in conjunction with the in-depth interview, to help us assess the candidates our search turns up. So for the Behavioral Characteristics portion of the position spec, we use terminology similar to the terminology we use in preparing the test results. Examples are as follows:

The degree to which the candidate is aggressive and domineering, as opposed to passive and unwilling to operate in an antagonistic environment.

The degree to which the candidate is outgoing and people-oriented, as opposed to introverted.

The degree to which the candidate is fast-paced and able to keep multiple balls in the air without becoming unduly stressed, as opposed to slow-paced, patient, deliberate, and methodical.

The degree to which the candidate is attentive to detail, rule-and-regulation-oriented, as opposed to being recalcitrant or perhaps looking at a rule and trying to figure out how to get around it.

What **values** drive the candidate? Is he money-motivated? Does an opportunity for promotion appeal to her? Would he be more motivated for an opportunity for a day off, or to be selected as a member of the company's employee advisory board?

How does the candidate make decisions? Is he more research-oriented, or does he rely more on his gut feelings? How important is it for the candidate to do her homework before making major business decisions?

How important is it to the candidate to live up to his commitments or achieve closure, to finish the things he starts? To what degree is she organized?

What is the candidate's risk-tolerance level? How well does he deal with change, or is he more comfortable with the status quo? Can she be relied upon to innovate new ways of doing things in the organization? Can he think well "on his feet"?

How well can she be relied upon to keep an eye on quality?

How effectively can she work indoors in a confining office environment without becoming unduly stressed?

As you refer to the position specification in Appendix I, jot down some references to the same psychological characteristics the tests measure and are revealed from the candidates' answers to the questions asked in the in-depth interview.

In-depth Interview

Referring to the answers in the in-house questionnaire, the job description, and the results the successful candidate must deliver, it is now time to design the in-depth interview questions. Using these questions, the in-depth interview should be conducted with each candidate who becomes a finalist.

Rules for Designing In-depth Interview Questions

As a rule of thumb, design each question so that it cannot be answered with a "yes" or a "no." Most questions should be open-ended in nature. Open-ended questions usually begin with phrases like:

- "Tell me about . . . "
- "Describe how you might . . . "
- "What are your favorite . . . ?"
- "In the past when you were faced with _____, how did you typically respond?"
- "If you were to be the successful candidate, tell me how you would deal with _____?"
- "If you were the successful candidate, how would you envision spending your first 60 days on the job to get off to the best start?" (This question is especially effective for sales candidates.)

Any time you ask a question that *can* be answered with either a yes or a no, follow up the question with a request for examples.

Let's say that one of your interview questions is, "How effective are you at taking business away from the competition without using price as a weapon?"

Odds are that the candidate's answer will be something along the lines of, "I think I'm excellent at bringing in new business."

So be prepared with a follow-up question such as, "Could you give me some examples of customers you brought to your present company and the techniques you used to take them away from the competition?"

By comparing the answers each candidate provides to the questions in the in-depth interview, management is in a much better position to make the best decision.

Rules for Conducting In-depth Interviews

With the candidate's permission, I suggest that you tape record the in-depth interview. With a $40 tape recorder and an inexpensive attachment from Radio Shack, you can capture the interview on tape. There are several benefits of doing this:

- You can share the tape with other members of your management team and receive their input.
- You can listen a second or third time to how the candidates answered key questions.
- You can compare how effectively multiple candidates answered the same interview question.
- You can avoid the travel expenses associated with bringing unqualified candidates to your place of business for additional evaluation.

Legal Considerations

In most states, it's legal to tape record a telephone interview as long as the other party is aware that the phone call is being recorded and gives their permission; however to be legally safe, you may wish to ask your attorney's opinion.

Set Specific Criteria for Evaluating the Successful Candidates' Progress

Once you decide on candidates and are successful at bringing them on board, it's important to agree with the candidates on what measurable goals they must achieve after the first 90 days, after the first six months, and after the first year. Only by setting measurable goals and monitoring how well the candidate is doing at meeting them will you be able to correctly evaluate his or her progress.

MANAGEMENT MISTAKE

Failure to Set Long-term Goals for the Business

If there's anything more important than addressing short-term business goals, it's preparing a strategic plan that will provide a road map for the organization to follow over the long term. While changes in the local, regional, national, or world economic picture may cause the strategic plan to be modified every year or two, strategic planning is critical for companies that wish to optimize business opportunities.

In the absence of a strategic plan, a business will tend to impulsively react to unforeseen obstacles and opportunities. Armed with a well-designed strategic plan, however, managers have the luxury of responding to various pressures that crop up in the day-to-day life of any organization in keeping with the company's long-term thinking.

One of my clients was expanding by attempting to acquire new locations when competitors offered their businesses for sale. Because there was no plan in place as to where the company would add locations, the company's geographic growth was sporadic. Availability in a particular geographic region was the number-one criterion, as opposed to market opportunity.

I knew a building material supplier who made the decision to build a truss and wall panel manufacturing plant. The investment in the land, building, and equipment was well over $1 million. The client's customer base, however, was relatively small custom builders, not national builders who are more inclined to use components in the building process. When the plant was ready to go into production, the CEO realized that his sales force was inadequate to service large national builders who were less likely to do business on a relationship basis. He lost tens of thousands of dollars as he struggled to hire a more sophisticated sales force that understood how to penetrate this customer base.

In writing a strategic plan for a business, it's critical to agree on how fast the management team and the board of directors wish to grow the business. By agreeing on a compounded growth rate, the door is open for all kinds of strategic decisions.

Among the following are questions that compounded growth projections will make it possible for decision makers to answer:

- At what point will we outgrow our existing facilities?

- At what rate will we "burn" our available capital?
- How much capital will we require to support the growth of our business?
- At what rate can the stockholders expect their investment in the business to grow?

Once the compounded growth rate is agreed upon, a strategic plan should answer the following questions:

1. Where are we going? What is our management team committed to accomplish in measurable terms, and over what time frame?
2. How are we going to get there?
3. What obstacles are we likely to face along the way? And how will we get around them?
4. What is our action plan?

Some companies can manage without preparing a strategic plan, but I believe that the highway to success is made much less bumpy and a lot less stressful when there is a plan in place. I've heard an analogy that says trying to manage a business without a plan is like going bird hunting and shooting up into the air in hopes that a bird flies in the path of your shot. The moral is that the odds of success are much greater when a company's strategic direction has been given enough thought to avoid too many guesses.

See Appendix V for a copy of a strategic planning questionnaire I have designed. By answering the questions, you'll be able to prepare a strategic plan for your business.

MANAGEMENT MISTAKE

Violating Lines
of Authority

This management mistake is easy to make, and it's especially prevalent in businesses founded by entrepreneurs. After all, in the early stages of an entrepreneurial enterprise, the founders call most of the shots. Founders may be doing much of the work themselves before the business grows to the size where additional staff joins the company.

As long as everyone on the business team reports to a single boss, lines of authority are pretty much impossible to violate. But when the first middle manager is hired, founders face their first challenge not to go around the newly hired manager and criticize or issue directives to employees who report to the new manager.

Violating lines of authority, however, takes place in virtually all companies I have worked with in my consulting practice, regardless of the age of the company. Managers rarely even realize that it's a major management faux pas.

On a consulting assignment with a business in Florida, I met with an owner who had started his business from scratch. He began with a handful of products that he purchased, sold, and delivered. He even did the collecting. He was the classic "one-man show" except for a free-lance bookkeeper who pulled together the paperwork well enough to keep the financial records in order.

As time passed, however, the business grew. He first hired a sales force and later a sales manager. Eventually, he brought a buyer on board. The business was beginning to take off.

The owner's biggest organizational issue was that he could never get out of the habit of answering questions from employees who reported to one of his subordinates. If he saw something he didn't like, he would violate his managers' lines of authority in a heartbeat by handing out directives to whomever happened to be standing nearby.

In many cases, his directives would fly in the face of conflicting instructions that had been issued by the employees' direct supervisors.

His best managers began to complain. The owner would apologize and promise to be more sensitive to the organizational structure he had designed, but time and time again he would fail to respect his own rules.

Then one day, the sales manager resigned, citing a specific event that became the straw that broke the camel's back. Apparently, the sales manager—who had pricing authority—refused to authorize a salesperson to reduce an established price. When the salesperson asked the owner for his advice, he told him, "Take the order. Let me deal with the sales manager."

This wasn't the first time such a violation had occurred. So the sales manager, feeling as if his authority had been usurped, quit.

Two months later, an incident occurred with an administrative employee, who had used all of her vacation days and sick leave. Her sister was getting married in Italy, so citing extenuating circumstances she asked the office manager for a week off. The office manager refused, saying that if she did take the time off, she could do so only as an unpaid leave of absence.

With several years' tenure, the administrative employee hit the ceiling, accusing the office manager of unfairness. In anger, she stormed into the owner's office. He made the same mistake he had made with the sales manager; he told her to go ahead and take the time off. "Let me deal with the office manager," he told her.

Humiliated, the office manager quit.

The frustrated owner hired me to work with him to reduce employee turnover, especially within management ranks.

He didn't have a clue. He didn't seem to realize that he was the problem. But once I interviewed the managers that reported to him, there was little doubt about what had to change before the organization could stop management flight.

What the owner failed to realize was that his managers were not developing; they weren't growing as managers.

Why? Because the owner was not only usurping their authority by violating their lines of authority, he was also requiring the managers to "check with him" before making key decisions.

At his company, we established minimum conditions of employment and pinpointed measurable accountability for each of the managers and for each of their reporting units where applicable. I say "where applicable" because there are some duties in certain positions that are very difficult to measure. Receptionists come to mind. Whereas it is easy to measure the number of calls processed over a given period of time, the primary responsibility of the receptionist is to make the caller feel like a million dollars and to process the call efficiently and effectively without making the caller feel rushed, and that's difficult to measure.

If managers are not allowed to make mistakes, they will never grow.

Order must exist within any organization for it to function efficiently and effectively. But a structured approach to managing people cannot develop if managers don't respect the organizational structure they've established. In a worst-case scenario, middle managers' authority is usurped, rendering the middle manager both a paper tiger (no teeth in the position) and ineffective as a manager.

But even when violating lines of authority is a part of a company's culture, some degree of operational chaos invariably develops up and down the organization.

Much of the blame for these scenarios should be placed squarely on the company's CEO, but human nature is a contributing factor, as well. It's not unlike children going to their mother with a question, and when they don't get the answer they want, going to their father to see if he will be more permissive.

When this behavior emanates from the rank and file, it's called "playing one manager against another." All managers, especially those who operate in close proximity to each other, must be aware of this tendency and make sure they're not being used to enable a subordinate to beat the system.

The number-one discipline all managers must embrace is to think twice before responding to a question from someone who does not report to them directly. As easy as this may sound, it isn't. Most managers are eager to help out by providing an answer.

Let's say a senior manager is walking through the company's assembly area and notices a pile of scrap material lying on the floor that could be a safety hazard. It takes discipline to resist stopping in his tracks, finding a shop foreman, and telling him to get the mess cleaned up.

The correct behavior, of course, is to make a note of the problem and tell the shop foreman's manager to ask the shop foreman to fix the problem. If the problem is serious enough, the senior manager can find a telephone or an intercom and make the request from the shop floor.

I often see lines of authority violated between the CEO or COO and the credit manager. After doing her homework, the credit manager decides to set a relatively low credit limit or outright deny credit to a particular customer. Then when the salesperson learns of the credit manager's decision, he goes over the credit manager's head to the boss.

The management mistake occurs when the boss yields to the salesperson's request and overrules the credit manager, thinking the risk is worth the amount of new business the new customer promises to bring to the table.

BETTER: The boss tells the salesperson that he will review the case. The boss then goes to the credit manager to get an idea of what her research revealed. If the boss decides that the credit manager was too conservative, he can discuss other options and allow her to approach the salesperson with any modification in her original decision.

BIGGEST PROBLEM: Any time a supervisor usurps a subordinate's authority, it is extremely difficult to hold that subordinate accountable for measurable results.

Take the case of the credit manager. Let's say she's paid a monthly bonus tied to average collection days and an annual bonus tied to bad debt expense versus budget. When the boss overrules the credit manager and approves a new account the credit manager rejected, and the decision comes back to bite the company, it's unfair to penalize the credit manager for the bad debt.

If the boss attends a trade show and makes the independent decision to put in a new product line, and the new line fails to sell, it's not fair to hold the company's buyer accountable for inventory turnover.

BETTER: When the boss feels strongly about something, discuss the issue, voice concerns, or even present some homework. But never violate a subordinate's lines of authority by taking the matter into your own hands.

MANAGEMENT MISTAKE

Asking Employees to Serve Two Masters

In small, poorly structured companies, employees are often asked to report to two or more supervisors.

When I conduct a consulting assignment, one of the first questions I ask is, "Who do you report to? Who is your direct supervisor?"

The answer is sometimes, "Well, that's a good question. When it comes to questions about company policy, I look to Ward Stephens, but to ask for a day off or do something special for a customer, I would report to Connie Jackson."

It's a poor management practice to ask an employee to serve more than one master; that is, to report to more than one supervisor.

Reporting to two supervisors can be a license to play one against the other. It's different, but it's similar to Management Mistake #6, Violating Lines of Authority. Again, it's like a child asking his mom for permission to visit a friend. If she says no, then he asks his dad, hoping that dad will say yes without touching base with mom. I believe any parent will understand what I'm referring to here.

The most efficient organizations make the lines of authority extremely clear. When they become blurred, so does efficiency.

I worked with a company in which the owner was also the CEO. When the CEO decided that he had too many middle managers to manage, he hired a general manager. He gave the GM authority over operations and purchasing, but he insisted that he—the CEO—and the GM share authority over the sales force.

If I had been the GM, I would have refused to participate in such an arrangement, but this particular GM was new to the company and didn't want to rock the boat, so he accepted the role as co-manager over the sales force.

When I was retained to conduct a consulting assignment at this company, I quickly uncovered unrest among the sales personnel. They were unbelievably frustrated. The GM would work with them to establish their priorities with each customer and each prospect, but the CEO, based on his own set of priorities, would often redirect one or more of the salespeople.

An example would be when a customer called the CEO to complain about the level of service he was receiving. The CEO would contact the salesperson assigned to the customer and tell him to drop whatever it was he was doing and fix the problem. The CEO never thought to touch base with the GM and ask him to take charge of fixing the problem; he went directly to the salesperson.

The GM—who may have directed the salesperson in an entirely different direction—would be infuriated when the salesperson ignored his instructions in favor of the CEO's command.

The unfortunate salesperson was caught in the middle; he couldn't possibly win. If he failed to switch priorities, he was in trouble with the CEO. If he ignored the GM's instructions and was obedient to the CEO, the GM would be upset with him.

The sad part of this scenario was that the CEO was oblivious to the problems his management style was causing. I had to convince the CEO that he was committing a major business management mistake.

I was guilty of this very management mistake when I hired my first general manager. The GM's job description called for all employees in our office to report to him. But as I had done ever since I founded the company, I would return from a consulting assignment and heap all kinds of work on our administrative assistant. I was oblivious to the fact that my GM had already established her priorities.

The solution was an easy one. My GM approached me and asked me very respectfully if I would be kind enough to modify my behavior and bring my priorities to him, and he would see that the administrative assistant met my deadlines. I complied, and the problem immediately went away.

ACTION PLAN: Take a look at your organization and determine if there are any employees who are set up to report to more than one supervisor. If you find some, fine-tune the lines of authority so that no employee has more than one direct supervisor.

DOTTED-LINE RELATIONSHIP: On many organizational charts you'll see a dotted line between various members of the business team. A dotted line between Supervisor A and an employee who reports to Supervisor B means that while Supervisor B is the employee's direct supervisor, Supervisor A has some degree of influence over this particular employee's position.

An example might be the relationship between the receptionist and the sales manager. The receptionist might report to the office manager, but because the receptionist is the first point of contact when customers call in, the sales manager may have some influence over the words the receptionist uses when answering the telephone, how calls are routed, etc.

In doing research on dotted-line arrangements in the workplace, I ran across the following explanation from Joan Lloyd and Associates, a Milwaukee-based management consultant and executive coach, in response to an inquiry her firm received:

INQUIRY: "When I was searching for information for my MBA thesis, I read a recent article of yours regarding co-managing. I'm having a little trouble finding research material on co-management or joint lead management. I was hoping you could point me in the right direction. I'm trying to find information about how to effectively co-manage technicians in the technology manufacturing sector. The company I work for has two managers for the technicians on the factory floor. One is an engineer, and one is an operations manager. Both represent the technicians when it comes to pay and promotions, etc.

"Are you aware of any other industries that use this type of management style? Do you know of any research that's been done on this style of management?"

LLOYD'S ANSWER: "This co-managing phenomenon occurs in situations where two specialties are required in one job. In your case, technicians need engineering expertise as well as operational know-how to produce a product. In other cases, sales professionals may need engineering expertise to sell a high-tech product. In health care, a radiologist, for example, may work in a special section of the hospital, delivering service to a special population.

"For example, I am working with an organization that has set up a special pediatric health center within the hospital. To staff the center, employees with special expertise were assigned from areas such as radiology and lab.

"These employees still report to their former managers in their own departments and don't formally 'report to' the new head of the pediatric center. As you might expect, the head of the center started to experience some difficulties when it came to trying to direct the activities of these employees since she had no real authority over them.

"The employees have two people to answer to— always a tricky situation. The center has specific goals, and the radiology department and other department heads have their own set of goals and commitments that their employees must meet. The employees are in the middle. And typically, the respective managers end up wrestling over resources.

"Sometimes a workable solution involves a 'solid-line' and a 'dotted-line' reporting relationship that is clearly defined. For example, in the case of the clinic employees, we determined that the clinic goals were more primary than the respective departmental goals for these employees. However, the employees were concerned about losing their technical expertise if they didn't have some connection to their specialty departments. How would they keep their skills up-to-date? Who could they ask for coaching on a tough case? How could they stay visible for other hospital opportunities?

"The solution seems to be in a negotiated relationship with both areas. For instance, the solid-line reporting relationship should be to the clinic, since their outcomes must be aligned with the vision and mission of the clinic. The head of the clinic should be able to direct their work, give them feedback, and have authority over how they spend their time.

"To meet the employees' needs for technical and career growth, they have a dotted-line reporting relationship with the department head of their specialty. This will ensure they will stay visible and viable and enable them to tap resources.

"The clinic head will consult the respective department heads when it comes to employees' performance reviews and ask for help with career development opportunities, such as directing an employee in a special research project.

"I believe that in order for this to work, the employee has to have one boss. In other words, while it sounds good in theory for an employee to have an operations manager and an engineering manager, in the end, one has to be primary. In your case, the operations manager may carry more weight, since he or she has the bottom-line responsibility for getting the product out the door. Trying to have two managers is more complicated, prone to conflict, and costly . . . "

MANAGEMENT MISTAKE

Failure to Prepare
a Succession Plan

All executives eventually leave the business, either voluntarily or involuntarily. Even if the owner or general manager refuses to establish a retirement date, name a successor, and pass the torch in an orderly manner, the torch will eventually be passed anyway. This transition may occur when the corporate leader loses his health or at the time of his death, but it will occur sooner or later.

Several years ago, I had a corporate client in Florida that was still managed by the founder. And although the founder was 86 years of age, he flatly refused to name a successor. He had two lieutenants who were in their sixties and capable of succeeding the founder, but he would never pull the trigger.

I'll call this founder Mr. Chapin (not his real name). "Mr. Chapin," I pleaded, "you know that you can't live forever. So for the sake of your heirs and your employees, don't you think it would be a wise decision for you to name a successor so the successor will have a few years under your tutelage while your health is still good?"

"Who's to say that I won't live forever, young man?" was Mr. Chapin's response to my plea.

When Mr. Chapin finally did pass the torch, it was only because he died of a sudden heart attack. The family scrambled trying to figure out what to do, but by this time about the only option they had available to them was to put the business on the market. And because there was no successor in place and because no forward thinking had occurred for so many years, the business brought only a fraction of the price it could have been sold for just a few years before.

RULE: By the time a CEO reaches the age of 55, it's time to announce to the board of directors a firm retirement date, even if that date is 10 years out in the future.

By announcing a retirement date, the CEO is forced to begin planning for an orderly succession. This process begins, of course, with the selection of a successor. *(See Appendix IV, Preparing a Position Specification.)*

If there are multiple succession candidates on board, the CEO has ample time to groom one or more of them for the top slot. If the CEO deems that there are no qualified successors currently on the payroll, he or she has the necessary time to recruit one.

Especially in family-owned and -managed businesses, it is difficult to attract high-quality talent into an organization in which the future of the company has not been planned. It has been my experience from managing my company's recruiting division that ambitious candidates frequently resist aligning themselves with organizations that haven't announced formal succession plans. If in Company A, the future is ambiguous, but in Company B the company's future has been clearly laid out, the best candidates almost always opt for Company B.

The quickest way to kill employee morale is to fail to provide a predictable work environment. It's human nature to want to know what's on the horizon, where the company is going, and who is going to lead it there. This is the reason it's important for owners and managers to take the time to prepare a succession plan.

The movers and shakers in the marketplace—the big producers, the men and women who possess the ability and the talent to make things happen for your company—are ambitious; they want to see an opportunity to move forward in whatever company they join. This single fact of human nature is the best argument I know of for both a long-range plan and a formal organizational structure. But this pitfall is present in many organizations—especially family-owned or private enterprises. It's a failure not only on the part of the CEO, but on the part of the management team in general, to prepare a succession plan.

Many of us want to work forever. Even allowing ourselves to think about retirement can be painful. But such thinking is selfish. I believe it's especially unfair to those in our respective organizations who have earned the right to vie for the top spot. Few worthy successors will stay with an organization that promises nothing more than a dead-end job.

In the interest of all parties involved—stockholders and employees—my boss in my old company required each of his reporting units to have a successor in place by a specific date. When the deadline I had agreed to came and I had failed to meet this goal, he tied one third of my next year-end bonus to my ability to name a qualified successor.

This got my attention.

We were told that if we didn't already have a qualified successor on board in our respective divisions, we were to recruit one. When you see this kind of thinking in an organization, you know you're dealing with a professionally managed firm.

I've never seen a company with too much talent. The opposite is more frequently the case. When an owner, general manager, or key executive suddenly dies, accepts a job with another company, or retires, so often there's no one on board to fill his or her shoes, slowing the company's momentum.

How about in your firm? Do you have a qualified successor in place? If not, do yourself and your company a favor and begin the recruiting process.

MANAGEMENT MISTAKE 9

Giving Preferential Treatment to Family Members

By their very nature, family businesses attract family members. From the day many founders opened the doors for the very first time, it is typical that they will begin thinking about how they can persuade offspring, siblings, nieces, and nephews to join the ranks of the newly founded family business. This is even more prevalent in Asian and Latin American countries than it is in Europe and North America.

Even in this era of multinational and international enterprise, family businesses still provide more employment opportunities than any other business entity. As a product of a family business myself, I am a strong advocate of family-owned, family-managed businesses.

If a family business grows and becomes very successful, there are typically not enough family members to fill all the positions that must be filled. Therefore, candidates from outside the family must be attracted and recruited.

Hiring qualified candidates is never easy, but it's impossible to retain employees if they believe they're competing for promotions against a stacked deck. And by a stacked deck, I mean when non-family employees perceive that family members receive preferential treatment.

In business, the quality of the people equals the quality of the organization. I don't care if the business is manufacturing, distributing, retailing, health care, or in the service sector, good people are necessary to achieve an optimal level of performance. Great people won't remain with an organization where the playing field is not level.

Our recruiting division placed a VP-level candidate with a client in New York state. This candidate (I'll call him Jim) had multiple opportunities to join several other organizations in his industry, but chose ZYZ Corporation because the owner was in his late fifties and was looking for a successor to take the helm in a few years.

Jim knew that the owner had a son in business school, but the owner assured him that the son wanted no part of the family business, so he had never given the son much serious thought. After receiving his MBA, the son joined a large national company and began to enjoy some success. In fact, he received two nice promotions in his first four years there.

After about five years with XYZ, Jim had gained the respect of the entire management team. Everyone assumed that he was Mr. Big's heir apparent. Life was good.

Then one day Jim was called into his boss' office to learn that the son who had had zero interest in joining the family business had changed his mind and would be coming on board at the first of the year. The CEO asked Jim to take charge of him and help him learn the business.

Jim immediately saw the writing on the wall. He knew he couldn't compete with the flesh and blood of the CEO to become the CEO's successor. Within a few months, Jim had accepted a position with a competitor.

When Jim left, XYZ lost two more key employees who were loyal to Jim and didn't want to work in a company that showed favoritism to family members. Mr. Big lost face in his own company while he and his son faced the daunting task of rebuilding some semblance of a management team.

RULE: The number-one family rule is to treat all offspring *equally*. Give them birthday and Christmas gifts of approximately the same value. Buy them clothes of similar quality and value. Show no favoritism among offspring.

RULE: When children become adults and join the family business, treat them *equitably*. Reward offspring based on their talent and the results they are able to achieve.

The quickest way to kill a family business is to treat offspring *equally* after they've joined the organization, rather than *equitably*. Here's an example:

I have a client company that is owned by two brothers. One brother never showed much interest in management, so the older brother became the CEO and managing partner. Following college, both of the older brother's sons joined the family business. The youngest managed a small manufacturing division while the older joined the purchasing division. Based on my experience with both of these offspring, I didn't believe either of them was qualified to succeed their father.

When the time came for the CEO to name a successor, he simply couldn't make a decision. His emotions were far too involved to risk family unity by choosing one son over the other or by going outside the company for a successor. As a result, he announced that the brothers would be co-presidents of the company. This, of course, was the beginning of the end. Under this dysfunctional arrangement, the organization began to go downhill, and the owner had no choice but to put the business up for sale.

Within a year, both boys were terminated by the acquiring company and had accepted mediocre positions with local competitors in the same industry.

ACTION PLAN: If you own or manage a family business, make sure that any family members who join the firm understand up-front that family members will be treated *equitably*.

MANAGEMENT MISTAKE 10

Paying Discretionary Bonuses

As a rule, any time I hear the word "discretionary" used to describe the way employee bonuses are arrived at, I smell trouble. The reason is because "at your discretion" opens the door for all kinds of emotional influences. The word "discretion" invites prejudice and bias. Here's how the Merriam-Webster Unabridged Dictionary defines discretionary: *Left to discretion; unrestrained except by discretion or judgment.*

In customer care seminars I conduct, I use the term "recency" curve to explain that the degree to which a customer is loyal to a company depends largely on what kind of customer service experience the customer had most recently with the company. When a loyal customer's confidence in your company is shaken because an employee treated him rudely, his loyalty diminishes, regardless of how many positive experiences the customer has had during previous visits.

The same is true of discretionary bonuses. When there is nothing tangible or measurable on which to base the amount of the bonus, there's a tendency for supervisors to recall their most recent experience with the employee.

If, for example, bonuses are paid out in January for the previous year, and a particular employee (one who had turned in a lackluster performance over the course of the year) landed a huge new customer in December, the discretionary bonus the supervisor approves is likely to be based on the December event.

On the other hand, let's say a sterling employee has performed handsomely over the course of the year, but in December, this same employee made an error in judgment that cost the company some money to fix. Odds are good that the supervisor will let that recent experience cloud her decision on how much to pay the employee in discretionary bonus.

RULE: Whenever possible, pay bonuses based on actual performance against predetermined goals and objectives.

Figure 1 below illustrates a bonus formula that can be used to calculate a bonus for an employee performing just about any job function. I call it the Double-Up/Double-Down Bonus Plan. I chose that name for the bonus plan because I have historically found it to be motivating to design the plan to increase and decrease at rapidly ascending and descending rates.

One of the beauties of the Double-Up/Double-Down Plan is its flexibility. The objective or the bonus may be manipulated in any way a manager chooses. The Double-Up/Double-Down Plan in Figure 1 is strictly an illustration, so don't read anything into the plan as a result of the way I have structured it.

Double-Up/Double-Down Incentive Plan Concept

This is a plan that works well for numerous positions in any industry. Examples are piece-rate incentives for manufacturing personnel, inventory turnover for buyers, average collection days for credit managers, operating expense goals for operations managers, return on assets or return on sales for general managers, and so on.

Here's the way the plan might work for a buyer. *Purely as an example,* I am assuming that this particular buyer has a performance objective of eight inventory turns annually.

FIGURE 1

Objective	Incentive
7.00–7.19 turns	-0-
7.20–7.39 turns	$200
7.40–7.59 turns	$400
7.60–7.79 turns	$600
7.80–7.99 turns	$800
8.00–8.19 turns	$1,000 (Objective)
8.20–8.39 turns	$1,400
8.40–8.59 turns	$1,800
No Limit	No Limit

As you can see, this plan is flexible. You can substitute any goal or objective and any incentive amount you choose. In this particular example—inventory turns—the incentive would be paid annually.

However, you could also design an incentive plan for, say, a credit manager, based on average collection days and pay the incentive monthly.

You could design an incentive plan for your operations manager to control, say, operating expenses as a percentage of sales in his area of responsibility. It could be paid either annually or monthly. Personally, I prefer to pay the incentive on a monthly basis whenever possible, or at least as close as possible to when the results—positive or negative—are achieved.

Figure 2 shows how this same incentive plan concept may be used to calculate a credit manager's monthly incentive compensation. To illustrate the plan's flexibility, I have arbitrarily chosen to increase and decrease the incentive in identical increments of $20.

FIGURE 2

Objective	Incentive
No Limit	No Limit
43 days	$140
44 days	$120
45 days (Goal)	$100 per month
46 days	$ 80
47 days	$ 60
48 days	$ 40
49 days	$ 20
50 days	-0-

Sales Compensation

Perhaps the easiest position to measure in any organization is a sales position. Salespeople are charged with the responsibility for selling more to existing customers and selling customers that currently do business with the company's competitors. As a result, more salespeople are paid on the basis of performance than any other position in the business world.

Sales Commissions

In most companies that make use of an outside sales program to move the company's goods and/or services, the sales manager assigns customers to the individual salespeople. In the accounts receivable module of the company computer system, a salesperson's name is assigned when the account is set up. The computer system can then calculate each salesperson's individual sales and gross profit results merely by adding the purchases of each of his or her assigned customers.

Most organizations I have worked with pay their road salespeople a monthly sales commission, which is a percentage of the sales or gross profit dollars they generate; but if the commission is calculated as a percentage of sales, the percentage is often tied to the gross margin (gross profit as a percentage of sales) each individual salesperson generates. The rate of commission will, of course, vary from industry to industry.

In distribution businesses, for example, commissioned salespeople usually earn a maximum of 2.5% to 3% of sales, or 10% to 15% of the gross profit their customers generate. Gross margins in this industry will usually range from the low to high 20% range.

In the used car business, however, salespeople frequently earn only minimum wage as a draw against commissions of around 25% of the gross profit their sales generate.

In my first job as a salesperson, I worked for a manufacturer and earned a different commission on each product group I sold. The actual commission varied according to the gross margin the company earned on each individual product line. On average, I earned approximately 1.5% of sales.

Salespeople who don't have individual customers assigned to them are often paid an hourly wage plus incentive compensation tied to either the sales or the gross profit they generate, and sometimes a combination of the two. What is critical in taking advantage of this method of compensation, however, is the ability to track the inside salesperson's sales and/or gross profit.

Another popular compensation plan for salespeople is to pay a salary (if the salesperson qualifies for a salary under the Wage and Hour Law) plus incentive pay tied to agreed-upon performance goals.

Managers should ask the company's labor lawyer to review each employee group's pay plan to make sure the company is not in violation of federal or state Wage and Hour Laws.

Such a plan might call for the salesperson to receive a salary of, say, $2,000 per month plus a monthly, quarterly, or annual bonus, the amount of which would be determined by how well he or she performed against measurable goals. The more the salesperson exceeds the agreed-to objective, the higher the bonus.

In a few companies, however, salespeople are paid a salary and a discretionary bonus. When this is the case, conditions are ripe for discrimination.

When I am asked to help a client company convert from a salary and discretionary bonus plan to a more equitable plan based on performance, I ask the sales manager to give me the following:

- A list of the salespeople.
- Each salesperson's sales and gross profit dollar production for the previous three years.
- Each salesperson's total annual income (salary and discretionary bonus) for those years.

By dividing the annual income each salesperson received by both the salesperson's sales and gross profit production, I am able to determine the degree of inequality that the discretionary bonus program has produced. And by the way, discretionary bonus plans are almost always inequitable; often they are substantially inequitable.

The following is an example:

FIGURE 3

Salesperson	Annual Income	Income as % of Sales	Income as a % of GP
Smith	$46,312	4.76%	16.98%
Schwartz	$52,097	4.23%	16.22%
Phillips	$66,876	3.82%	15.75%
Jablanski	$73,822	3.02%	13.96%
O'Reilly	$96,386	2.86%	12.02%

In the example in Figure 3, Smith has been with the company for 24 years, receiving a discretionary raise in salary and discretionary bonus in each of those years. O'Reilly, on the other hand, has been with the company only four years, but is the company's biggest sales producer. But because of the discretionary system that has been in place for so long, Smith earns more as a percentage of sales and of gross profit than any of the other salespeople, not because of superior productivity, but because of tenure. Management never intended to discriminate; the discrimination is merely a result of a discretionary system of compensation.

Figure 4 illustrates an equitable system of sales compensation that is tied to both sales dollars and the gross margin each salesperson produces.

How to Remedy an Inequitable Discretionary Bonus Plan

This is no easy task, so obviously it is best—if you have a choice—to avoid the discretionary bonus habit altogether; but if you inherit such a plan, here's a way to convert to an equitable bonus plan based on performance.

At the beginning of your next business year, call a management meeting and announce to your middle managers that there will be no raises or discretionary bonuses this year, but you are going to give them a way to earn more money. Then announce the measurable goals each individual must achieve to earn a bonus. The Double-Up/Double-Down bonus concept will work for most employees.

FIGURE 4

SALES COMPENSATION PLAN TIED TO GROSS MARGIN	
Monthly Gross Margin Achieved	Commission as % of Sales
Below 13%	Negotiable
13.0–13.99	1.0
14.0–14.99	1.2
15.0–15.99	1.3
16.0–16.99	1.5
17.0–17.99	1.7
18.0–18.99	1.9
19.0–19.99	2.1
20.0–20.99	2.3
21.0–21.99	2.5
22.0–22.99	2.7
23.0–23.99	2.9
24.0–24.99	3.1
25.0–25.99	3.2
26.0–above	3.3
Gross Margin on Sales Shipped Directly to Jobs	
5.0–8.0	7.5
Over 8.0	9.0

The next step is to coach your middle managers on how to present this new bonus information to their direct reports. Arm them with the answers to the questions they are likely to receive from the people who report to them.

For employees whose jobs are difficult to measure (receptionists, accounts payable clerks, secretaries, janitorial staff, etc.), consider tying their bonus to the company's ability to achieve its sales or bottom-line profit goal.

WARNING: If you do tie any bonuses to your company's bottom-line profit goals, I caution top management not to take personal liberties with the company's income statement that will make employees feel that their bonuses are being negatively affected—otherwise negative attitudes are almost certain to develop.

ACTION PLAN: If you have employees in your organization who are paid a discretionary bonus, seriously consider a way to convert them to a bonus schedule that is based on performance against agreed-to goals and objectives.

11
MANAGEMENT MISTAKE

One Rule for Owners,
Another for Employees

In my dad's business, we had a gasoline tank for the purposes of refueling our delivery vehicles. My dad and his partners and their immediate family members allowed themselves to refuel their personal automobiles at the "company gas pump." We abided by a strict rule, however. Immediately following the refueling process, the family member was to go directly to a log book and jot down the number of gallons and value of the gasoline that had been pumped into a personal vehicle.

My dad knew that if employees saw owners taking advantage of the system—that is, pumping gasoline and failing to pay for it—that they would feel entitled to the same privilege.

In later years, when I was a member of the management team at BMA, we employed as our director of security a former FBI agent, Mr. Tom Dyer. Dyer was a world-class security expert who provided security services to our customers who had perhaps experienced an inventory shortfall they couldn't explain or some other type of internal theft. It was Dyer's job to find the thief or do whatever else was necessary to fix the security problem.

Dyer was a master interviewer. I was always amazed to see how quickly and effectively he could persuade the guilty party to confess to dishonesty.

On numerous occasions Dyer would tell me that the employees would make statements such as the following as their excuse for stealing:

"Yeah, I stole gas for my personal car, but why shouldn't I? I must have seen the owner's son do it a hundred times."

"Yes, I took material out of stock and delivered it to my home. But why shouldn't I? I know for a fact that the owner built his entire house out of company inventory he never paid for. How do I know? He told me."

"Yes, I put cash in my pocket and not in the cash register. Why? First of all, I haven't had a raise in two years, so I figured the company owed me a lot more than I took. But I'll tell you another thing, when the owner would take a business trip to Las Vegas, I've seen him clean out the cash drawer and use company money to gamble with."

RULE: All thieves can—at least to themselves—justify or make excuses for their dishonesty.

RULE: If owners and managers expect to prevent employee theft and reduce poor employee morale, they must understand human nature well enough to realize that employees will justify stealing, especially when they see owners or managers stealing. It's something like, "If he can do it and get away with it, why shouldn't I?"

These examples are intended to emphasize that owners and managers should not be surprised if their own behavior is modeled by observant employees. So I encourage management to take the following precautions:

- When an owner or manager takes material home from a retail business, make it crystal clear that an invoice was issued.

- When a member of the management team uses, say, a company credit card on a business trip, make it obvious to administration workers that any personal expenses are reimbursed by seeing that a personal check accompanies the expense report.

- Put yourself through Dr. Frank Bucaro's "ethics check" (www.frankbucaro.com) with everything you do and with every decision you make. Here are a few of the questions you must ask yourself to avoid using the power of your position to engage in or authorize unethical conduct:
  1. Is it legal?
  2. Would I be embarrassed if what I am about to do was published in the local newspaper?
  3. Would I be embarrassed if my family knew that I was engaging in this activity?

4. Would I be embarrassed if what I was doing
    was posted on the company bulletin board?

It's a good rule to assume that everything you do will
be found out by someone in your company. There are
just too many eyes and ears, too many checks and bal-
ances, to think any differently. My experience has taught
me to walk the straight and narrow when it comes to
making business decisions. Don't give your people any
excuse to justify dishonest behavior.

ACTION PLAN: Publish a written policy that details the
systems and procedures each owner, manager, and
employee is expected to follow for any behavior that
could be perceived as impropriety.

(See Chapter 29 on Ethical Standards.)

MANAGEMENT MISTAKE

Failure to Accept
Personal Accountability

Until managers are willing to step up to the plate and accept personal accountability for their failures, they run the risk of not only sounding pathetic, but losing the respect of their entire business team.

Notice that I said "accept personal accountability for their failures"; I did not include successes. The reason is because it's not much of a challenge to take credit for successes, but when it comes to failures, there's a strong tendency for them to become someone else's fault.

How many times have you read in the business section of the newspaper or in a public company's annual report the CEO's explanation for lower-than-anticipated earnings? You'll almost always find that external events beyond the CEO's control are given to the press and stockholders. Here are some examples:

- Softness in the economy did not allow us to achieve anticipated sales goals for the year.
- Rapidly rising fuel costs caused our operating expenses to rise more than we anticipated.
- The Teamsters' unwillingness to negotiate a satisfactory labor package reduced our earnings over the last year.
- Unfavorable weather conditions reduced demand for our products.
- The strength of the U.S. dollar affected our ability to compete in the Western European market.

Can you imagine a baseball player who just struck out at the plate blaming someone other than himself for his failure to get on base?

How about a basketball player who missed a shot at the buzzer blaming someone other than himself for failing to hit the basket?

Have you ever heard a golfer who hit a drive into the water blaming someone other than herself for failing to hit the fairway?

Nine times out of ten, when a business performs poorly, I believe the manager should be held fully accountable. After all, it's the manager who calls the shots. It's the manager who is supposed to make the necessary adjustments when economic conditions call for a change in strategy.

- Managers either hire all employees or else they hire the managers who make hiring decisions, so top management must take responsibility for the performance of the personnel on the business team. As mentioned earlier in this book, the quality of the people in an organization equals the quality of the company.

- Managers control the company's policies for dealing with customers, vendors, and employees.
- Managers oversee the purchasing department.
- Managers oversee the credit department.
- Managers oversee the financial and administrative areas of the company.
- Managers participate in designing the company's marketing plan.

I could go on and on, but think I've made my point. If you can't point your finger at the manager, then who would you point it toward?

Middle managers down through the rank and file look to the company's leaders for clues as to how they should behave. When they see the top management team pointing their fingers in the direction of someone other than themselves, the message is received loud and clear that passing the buck is an accepted practice.

ACTION PLAN: Set the standard in your company or department by accepting full responsibility for the successes and failures that occur as a result of the decisions you make.

MANAGEMENT MISTAKE

Failure to Gain Outside Exposure

Business owners and managers who spend too much time in their own business are guilty of breathing their own exhaust; that is, they too rarely gain exposure to new, different, or better ways of getting things done.

Several years ago, I was exposed to a successful business owner in Eugene, Ore. The owner had hired my company to conduct a recruiting assignment for a merchandising manager for his firm, a local consumer-oriented building materials company. So to better understand the culture we were hiring into, I traveled to Oregon to visit the operation. In the course of the visit, the owner told me that each year he budgeted more than $50,000 in travel expenses to give his people exposure to what was going on in other regions in North America. "We don't see Eugene as a mecca for merchandising ideas," he told me.

I was impressed. That was in 1993; I wonder how much the owner spends in today's dollars. But I do know one thing about this business. The management team has successfully competed with Home Depot at Home Depot's game: selling building materials to consumers. While Home Depot has taken the consumer portion of most local lumberyards' business, this particular business has continued to grow and prosper.

Many times, exposure is the difference between success and super success for business owners.

I believe I have prospered as a consultant in no small degree as a direct result of my exposure to so many different businesses. In just about every week of my 40-year business career, I have visited several diverse businesses. If I picked up just one idea from each of the businesses I have visited, think of the number of ideas I have at my disposal to share with my clients.

I recommend to my clients that each year they budget both the money and the time to get outside their own business and visit with non-competing businesses like their own. Your only criteria is to select businesses to visit that do a better job than you do in some particular aspect of the business.

Maybe it's a business that does a better job than your company does at utilizing its computer system.

Maybe it's a business that puts substantially more margin on its bottom line than your company earns.

Maybe it's a business that has a more efficient dispatching and delivery system than your company does.

Maybe it's a business that controls its manufacturing costs better than you do in your business.

I can guarantee this: if you'll take this advice, you'll be a better manager.

ACTION PLAN: Make a list of non-competing businesses in your industry that are more efficient or that put significantly more money on the bottom line than you do. Next step: plan at least four visits per year to see firsthand what these businesses are doing differently than you're doing in your business.

MANAGEMENT MISTAKE 14

Failure to Train

If you think training is expensive, how much do you think ignorance is costing you?

I'm always amazed at how little money most managers budget for training. Yet virtually all businesses spend more expense dollars on salaries and wages than any other expense category. Businesses that earn less than an optimal bottom-line profit can almost always attribute the failure to optimize earnings to the relationship between personnel-related expenses and the productivity of those employees.

Training enhances your investment in your people in much the same way that repairs and maintenance enhance your investment in rental property. No one is as good as he or she can be, so to improve productivity, people must be exposed to ideas and techniques to enhance their productivity.

I spent eight years in purchasing. I worked hard. I wanted to do well, but without some quality training programs, I could not have realized my full potential. Over those eight years, I attended a dozen seminars on negotiating strategies, inventory management, and selling skills. Without this kind of specialized training, I would have left literally millions of dollars on the table. Manufacturers had invested in a huge number of training programs for their sales force, so without training, I would have been vulnerable to negotiating and sales tactics I would not have known how to respond to—a babe in the woods.

When my old company would enter a major negotiation with a key vendor, our negotiating team would spend at least a dozen hours preparing our game plan. And many times—especially with unsophisticated vendors who had not invested in training for their personnel—we would annihilate them at the negotiating table. They would exit their corporate jet talking about football, and we'd have just left a negotiating strategy session. These kinds of vendors, the ones who took their jobs too casually, never had a fighting chance. As the great businessman and author Jim Rohn says, "Taking your business too casually can make a casualty of your business."

There were other vendors, however, who were totally prepared, and this was where our training really paid off. Football coach Joe Paterno famously said, "The will to win is important, but the will to prepare is vital."

Another key area in which many companies fail to invest is how to most effectively work trade shows. Companies invest many thousands of dollars on trade show exhibits, transporting their people to work these events and entertaining customers while they're there. Yet rarely is one dollar invested in teaching the men and women working the trade show how to get optimal results. If your trade show personnel had more training, they would be much more effective while there.

Sales training is perhaps the worst failure I observe time and time again. In my consulting practice, I frequently ask salespeople to describe to me their strategy for taking business away from the competition. Based on the thousands of answers I've heard over the years, quoting low-ball prices or trying to "buy" the business heads the list.

"But doesn't this tactic have a negative effect on your gross margin?" I ask.

"Yes, it does temporarily. But after I've gotten the prospect on board with us because they're so eager to save money, I plan to slowly ease the price up. In no time I'll be back at my full [gross] margin."

How to Cook a Frog

Every time I hear a salesperson try to justify the low-ball quote strategy, it reminds me of the story about cooking a frog. You see, if you toss a frog into a pot of boiling water, the frog will immediately jump out of the pot. But if you put the frog into a pot of cold water and turn up the heat, the frog will be cooked before he is aware of what's happening to him. Trying to fool a prospect by quoting low-ball prices makes just about as much sense.

Selling is persuading. Selling is convincing. Selling is doing something for the prospect to earn his or her business. Selling is not cutting the price. Using this kind of unprofessional tactic is one the main reasons so many industries are having a difficult time raising their gross margin. Unless salespeople are trained in the art of selling, they will forever take the path of least resistance; that is, they will cut the price.

Most companies invite manufacturer or distributor salespeople to conduct product training for their salespeople, a practice I wholeheartedly endorse. I have one suggestion, however, that will make these programs have a more lasting effect. Invest in a digital video camera and record each program. Store the video recordings in a secure place so that future salespeople you bring on board can review them. This practice will speed up the learning process for new salespeople and provide easy access for veteran salespeople who wish to review the training session.

ACTION PLAN: Identify the personnel in your company who would benefit from additional training, and design a training program for each group. Keep accurate records as to how these individuals perform both before and after being exposed to training programs.

FIGURE 5

National Training Firms to Consider
Dale Carnegie Training for Groups and Individuals: www.dale-carnegie.com
American Management Association: www.amanet.org/index.htm
Customer Service Training: www.lisaford.com
Local Chamber of Commerce: (see local telephone directory)
Sales & Management Training: www.timconnor.com
Sales Training: www.meisenheimer.com
Sales Management Training: www.meisenheimer.com
Sales Training: www.leeresources.com
Business-to-Business Telephone Sales: www.businessbyphone.com
Ethics Training: www.frankbucaro.com
Business Etiquette Training: www.brodycommunications.com
Boosting Employee Morale: www.drzimmerman.com
Small Business Sales & Marketing: www.markleblanc.com

MANAGEMENT MISTAKE

Failure to Manage
the Balance Sheet

Inventory and accounts receivable make up around 80% of the assets in most businesses. And the more rapidly the sales of the business grow, the more capital the business will require to finance additional inventory and additional accounts receivable.

Current Ratio

The current ratio (current assets divided by current liabilities) measures the ability of a business to meet its monthly obligations. Depending upon how many inventory and accounts receivable turns the business is able to achieve, the current ratio will vary, but in many businesses I work with, a current ratio of two to one is typically required; that is, two parts current assets and one part current liabilities. Businesses that opt to offer extended credit terms to their customers will naturally require a higher current ratio than one that is involved exclusively in cash sales.

A business, for example, that turns its inventory six times per year and on average collects its accounts receivable every 60 days will require approximately a two-to-one current ratio in order to pay its bills every 30 days. If, however, inventory turnover is slower than six times per year, or if average collection days are greater than 60, the business will need a higher current ratio than two to one.

Inventory Management

When I interview buyers on consulting assignments, I often ask this question: "How is your job measured?"

The answer is rarely anything specific, but more often something like, "The biggest way for me to get in trouble with my boss is to run out of material. When that happens, everyone screams at me." So the best way for buyers to stay out of trouble is to maintain such a high level of inventory that they rarely run out of stock merchandise.

A buyer should be measured on some combination of the following results:

- Inventory turnover against plan.
- Performance of new product lines purchased.
- Elimination of "dead" inventory.
- Gross margin.

Inventory turnover is at the top of the list for one primary reason: unless inventory turnover is improved, a company's investment in inventory will increase at precisely the same rate that sales increase. This statement does not take into consideration inflation or deflation. So when a company's sales increase by 20%, inventory investment will also rise by 20% unless the buyer improves inventory turnover.

Here's one of the best questions for buyers to ask themselves when analyzing a particular sku or a group of skus: What are we doing with a two-month supply of this sku when our lead time from our vendor is only two weeks? Answering this question can help bring inventory quantity in line with anticipated lead times.

Another benefit of an emphasis on inventory turnover is to make buyers less likely to overbuy at trade shows when vendors are offering special dating programs. While the company does save the interest expense when it doesn't have to pay for merchandise for, say, six months, all of the other costs of carrying inventory must still be taken into consideration. This includes costs such as:

- Obsolescence
- Handling
- Insurance
- Damage
- Taxes

Buyers who are unaware of these additional inventory carrying costs may not take them into consideration and may overbuy to take advantage of dating programs.

Accounts Receivable

Credit management is a profession and should be managed by professionals. Most owners and managers are making a big mistake when they try to save money on salaries by handling the credit function themselves. Another risk owners and managers take when they manage credit is getting their emotions involved with customers who are also personal friends. Most owners and managers report that they have been bitten by a buddy they allowed to violate the company's credit policies and rules.

The most effective personality type for the job of credit manager is a person who is very attentive to detail and is, when necessary, willing to suspend a past-due customer's credit, albeit in a professional manner. Hard-nosed credit managers may have difficulty saying no to a good customer, but at the same time, they must do so in such a way that they can retain the customer's good will.

Like inventory, accounts receivable will increase in proportion to sales increases unless the credit manager is successful at reducing average collection days. Therefore, average collection days are the number-one measurement for a credit manager. Bad debt expense against plan is a close second.

Perhaps the most distasteful aspect of managing a business is lacking sufficient capital to keep up with the growth of the business. When capital is insufficient, it is difficult to take advantage of prompt pay discounts and meet payroll and other monthly obligations. Ultimately, a severe capital shortage will cripple a business to the point that it struggles just to maintain the status quo.

Real Estate

Owners and managers who struggle to find the capital for inventory and accounts receivable might be wise to lease rather than own their land and buildings. After all, most businesses are not in the real estate business; they're in a business that needs land and buildings to function, so renting land and buildings preserves capital for current assets.

Equipment

The same is true for businesses that require manufacturing equipment, racking, computers, delivery equipment, and so on. By leasing equipment, managers preserve capital for inventory and accounts receivable.

Purchasing used as opposed to new equipment is another option that can preserve capital.

Bankers

There are only two sources of capital for either a business or an individual: earnings and debt. The greater the earnings a business is able to generate, the less it will have to rely on its borrowing power. But when earnings fall short of expectations, most businesses will be required to either fork out additional capital from their personal bank account or else pay a visit to their friendly banker.

Bankers tell me that they prefer for a business to earn 60% of the capital the business requires to support its growth. When a business is successful at earning 60% of the capital it needs to grow, bankers will typically lend the business the other 40% required.

I recommend that my clients do business with a minimum of two banks. If you currently only do business with one bank, consider opening a payroll account with a second bank.

Why? The personal relationship a manager develops with a local banker can vanish if the bank merges or sells to another bank. This happened to me a few years back. I had a $1 million real estate mortgage with Life of Virginia that was up for renewal. The mortgage rate was no longer competitive, so I asked for and received a verbal commitment from a banker friend who was a lending officer with our lead bank when I was a corporate officer at my old company. I know I should have gotten the agreement in writing, but I had done business with this particular bank for 20 years.

About 30 days before my loan at Life of Virginia was due to terminate, my buddy lost his job when his bank sold out to a larger bank. I was left out in the cold. Fortunately for me, I had another relationship with the president of a start-up bank I was able to call upon.

So do business with a minimum of two banks. Access to capital is too critical to take chances.

ACTION PLAN: If you're not paying attention to your balance sheet, appoint your controller or CFO to pay attention to it for you. The better you manage your balance sheet, the more capital you'll have to support your company's growth.

MANAGEMENT MISTAKE

Failure to Prepare a
Formal Marketing Plan

At some point, most businesses decide that to achieve the company's sales and gross-margin goals, a formal marketing plan must be hammered out. Too few businesses take this step before slumping sales make it necessary.

Frequently, the great majority of a company's marketing plan is made up of its sales force, either inside or outside. But it's important to recognize that salespeople are far more effective when they're supported by marketing efforts that give them an edge when they're in front of customers.

While a *strategic* marketing plan identifies the classes of trade the company plans to market to, a formal marketing plan identifies the marketing tools the company will use to gain customers' and prospects' favorable attention.

I was recently approached by a 100-year-old company that had been very successful at sustaining sales increases year after year without any marketing effort whatsoever over and above its sales force. But suddenly, the company's sales were not keeping up with the growth of the market, and the company was losing market share. So the CEO felt pressure to develop a marketing plan to support his outside sales professionals.

The following are a few of the marketing activities I have found to be effective among my client base:

Educational Seminars

Many years ago, when I was responsible for my company's purchasing programs, I was invited by one of our largest vendors to attend a series of concurrent seminars presented at a hotel in a major city. The event, which was attended by more than 100 of this national manufacturer's customers, was one of the most effective marketing techniques I've ever observed. I was given the privilege of listening to several extremely bright experts explain what changes I could make in the way I did business to put more money on the bottom line.

As I discussed in Chapter 14, many managers resist spending the expense dollars to educate not only themselves, but also other members of their management team. Most managers realize they should devote more time and money to educating their people, but they fail to do so because they believe they're too busy to organize the curriculum. Making education a part of the marketing effort creates a win-win all the way around.

ACTION PLAN: Identify experts who can help your customers solve their most pressing business problems. Hire one or more to present seminar programs for your customers and prospects.

It's not enough to merely send out a notice to your customers and prospects inviting them to attend an educational event. Challenge your salespeople to get the lion's share of their customers and prospects to the seminar, as well. You can add enthusiasm by making the sign-up effort a contest, with prizes going to the winners.

MARKETING IDEA: Use placards to organize seating at the seminar. If possible, seat loyal customers next to key prospects. If the loyal customer and the prospect know each other, all the better. This gives the loyal customer all day to answer questions and sing the praises of your company.

This marketing idea is not just for customers. Have your key managers and entire sales force attend the seminar, as well. Again, using placards, intersperse employees among customers and prospects. At coffee breaks and at lunch, make sure key managers spread themselves around and spend time with key customers and prospects.

When you can help customers and prospects solve their most pressing business problems, make more money, or be more successful, they will beat a path to your door.

Incentive Travel

One of the most effective marketing plans is an incentive travel program. These programs are designed to reward customers when their purchases reach a designated level with a nice trip. There's no doubt about it, incentive travel programs are effective. They work. They can also be expensive, so it's important that they be set up correctly to optimize the opportunity to get more business from existing customers and to take some business away from the competition.

INCENTIVE TRAVEL BENEFITS: 1.) To motivate your customers and prospects to buy more from your company. 2.) To provide an opportunity to build memories and solid relationships among you, your key personnel, and your customers. I have clients who believe they have benefited so much from incentive travel programs that they have continued to offer them year after year.

LOCATIONS: Fun-and-sun locations tend to be effective, especially for customers who perhaps would resist spending the money to visit an exotic location on their own. Fun-and-sun venues in Las Vegas or perhaps beach settings in the Caribbean or Mexico are also among the most economical destinations, giving the company a lot of bang for the marketing buck.

Destinations in Europe can be costly and include the added complications of language barriers. But if you have a sophisticated customer base, European travel can be quite impressive.

Unless you have a person in your organization who has had a lot of experience with managing incentive travel programs, I strongly suggest that you retain a travel agency that specializes in incentive travel. First of all, an agency that knows the ropes should be able to actually save you money, but more importantly, it's critical that you know that your key customers and prospects are in the hands of professionals. You are a pro at what you do for a living, so hire a pro to take care of your incentive travel program.

MARKETING IDEAS: There are several rules I recommend to raise the odds that you will get the most mileage from your incentive travel program:

PROGRAM DESIGN: Put together an incentive travel program that will motivate your customers and prospects to do more business with you. This is typically done by assigning x number of points for each dollar of purchases. More points may be earned when the customers purchase product lines that yield significantly higher gross margins or target product categories. If customers are currently giving you 100% of their business, you might as well accept the fact that the incentive trip will be a gift to them. You can't get any more than 100% of a customer's business.

Have several people review your plan to make sure there are no loopholes that will end up costing you more than you budgeted for the program.

SUGGESTION: For what I hope are obvious reasons, your goal is to include on your trip as many customers and prospects as you possibly can, so it's a good idea to allow a "buy in." By "buy in," I mean that for customers who fall short of the goal, there is a provision in the program that allows them to pay out of their own pocket whatever portion of the trip they fail to earn.

KICKOFF DINNER INVITATION: Send an invitation to Mr. and Mrs. at the home address. Yes, it may cost double to include the spouse at the kickoff dinner, but in many cases it's the spouse who has the most influence when it comes to qualifying for the trip. Hold the kickoff dinner in a private room at a relatively upscale restaurant.

KICKOFF DINNER: The kickoff dinner announces the promotion. At the dinner, present a first-class slide show of the destination. If this is your first trip to this destination, you should be able to get a DVD from the resort you will be visiting. But if you've taken your customers on incentive travel trips in the past, you can show photographs from previous trips. Customers enjoy seeing themselves and reminding themselves of how much fun they had on last year's trip.

Just as with educational seminars, don't leave the seating at your kickoff dinner to chance. It's a good idea to strategically seat prospects, loyal customers, salespeople, and managers. Brainstorm among yourselves who you believe would be most effective seated next to whom.

INCENTIVE STATUS REPORTS: Send monthly status reports to Mr. and Mrs. at the home address. The status report should let the customer or prospect know how many points they have earned and what additional purchases they need to make to qualify for two free spaces on the trip.

DURING THE INCENTIVE TRIP: Assign several in-house amateur photographers to take photographs. At special events, put a couple of disposable cameras on the table or hand them out to participants. At next year's kickoff dinner, these photos will help to remind everyone how much they enjoyed the trip.

Educational Newsletter

One of my favorite definitions of marketing is to *be on the customer's mind when the customer is ready to buy.* Your company will be thought of in a favorable light any time you can share ideas with your customers and prospects that will let them know that you care about them and are trying to help them improve their profitability.

It's possible that a custom-imprinted educational newsletter may be available from consultants who work exclusively in your industry. If not, you can produce your own. Just be sure that the ideas you include in the newsletter are good ones for the purpose of helping your customers and prospects be more successful at their profession.

Get Customers on Your Turf

Look for opportunities to invite customers and prospects to visit your place of business. Open houses, product demonstrations, cookouts, mini trade shows, golf outings, picnics for customers and their families, perhaps with Olympic-type competitive events, etc., are often effective.

Relationships

Most businesses are based on relationships, so proactive steps to foster better customer relationships is a worthwhile objective of your marketing activities. If your customers come in and out of the market on a relatively frequent basis, your odds of earning a piece of each customer's business increase as your relationships improve.

MANAGEMENT MISTAKE

Throwing the Same Pitch to Every Batter

No self-respecting manager would encourage a sales-person to treat each customer exactly alike. Similarly, managers make a major mistake when they use the same managerial tactics on each of their reporting units, regardless of the individual's personality.

Vince Lombardi, the late great coach of the Green Bay Packers, was notorious for his heavy-handed coaching style. However, in an interview with a reporter, Lombardi admitted that he never used an abrasive style with a player unless the player could take it. Lombardi knew that different coaching styles worked for different players.

If you don't use psychological assessments to help you understand what type of managerial style works best with each of the men and women who report to you, you're missing out on a valuable management tool. Psychological testing is inexpensive, and it's accurate at assessing an individual's behavioral style.

While a more passive subordinate may be intimidated by an abrasive managerial style, a more domineering individual is often energized by the more aggressive style.

One employee may respond best to verbal instructions, while another may respond best to written communication.

A kick in the seat of the pants may motivate one employee, while another is best encouraged by a pat on the back.

Some employees are slow, deliberate, and methodical, while others are fast-paced and impatient.

Odds are you have some people reporting to you who are very attentive to detail, while others shoot from the hip.

If managers are able to mirror each of their direct report's learning styles, they will be more effective in getting the most productivity out of each person. I believe it's the manager's responsibility to use whatever managerial style gets the most out of each employee.

For the first six years of my career, I had enjoyed some successes in sales and to some extent in management, but I was never able to really break out and see my career soar. I had gotten into some bad management habits that prevented me from realizing my full potential. While I had some natural talent to draw upon, I needed a manager to take a personal interest in me and help me overcome some of the handicaps that were holding me back from a higher level of success.

In 1969, I changed jobs and began reporting to a manager who got out of me more productivity than any manager had ever gotten out of me in the past. He did it by caring enough about me to use managerial tactics that pinpointed the specific issues I was having to deal with as a result of my psychological makeup.

In this job, my career really took off. I give my boss full credit for not giving up on me and for having the wisdom to use managerial tactics with me that got results.

ACTION PLAN: Make a list of each of the people who report to you and determine which managerial tactics are most effective for each. List the behaviors to avoid when communicating with each of your employees.

MANAGEMENT MISTAKE

Failure to Inspect
What You Expect

Even the best and most effective managers must rely upon their people to execute business directives. Half the battle is communicating the results you want from your direct reports, but a lot of managers make the mistake of stopping there. To be sure you get the results you're looking for by the deadline you've established, it's critical that your people know that you will follow up—that you will inspect what you expect.

How many parents would allow their son to drive the family car on a date for the first time without first establishing a time for him—and the car—to return home? Probably not many. And how many of those same parents would go on to bed just like on any normal evening without staying up to make sure that the child had returned home safely? Probably even fewer.

Most parents check behind their offspring to make sure they've performed their chores according to the parents' specifications. But so often, managers forget this valuable lesson when delegating tasks and other responsibilities to their people.

One of the reasons an inspection of the work is so important is because quite often the manager will be expecting a certain set of standards to be adhered to, while the employee may have his or her own set of standards. So unless the project is communicated in no uncertain terms, managers are wise to follow up.

While on a consulting assignment recently, I overheard a store manager instruct his operations manager to inspect each delivery vehicle before allowing it to leave on a delivery. The company had been experiencing an inordinate number of back orders, so the manager wanted the operations manager to double-check behind each driver to make sure that the material on each delivery matched the material on the delivery ticket.

The manager assumed that the operations manager would begin immediately with the very next delivery truck that pulled up to the gate. But the next morning, several salespeople were lined up in the store manager's office complaining of more back orders.

When the manager called the operations manager to find out what had gone awry, he told him that he had gotten busy with another project and failed to initiate the inspection process.

Who was at fault?

The operations manager was certainly at fault, because he allowed another project to prevent him from following a direct order from his boss.

But the store manager was also at fault for failing to follow a basic management principle—he failed to inspect what he expected.

ACTION PLAN: Soon after you issue a directive to one of your people, get into the habit of following up to make sure the directive is being carried out to your satisfaction.

MANAGEMENT MISTAKE

Entitlement Programs Kill Productivity

In articles I've written over the years, I have used the phrase "laissez-faire," a term more frequently used to characterize governments than businesses, to describe a rather laid-back management style. When I use this term, I am referring to management personnel who put very little pressure on employees to achieve their full potential by pushing them toward peak performance levels.

Laissez-faire managers would much rather maintain a stress-free relationship with their personnel than face the antagonistic environment that sometimes arises when employee confrontations become necessary. They rarely turn up the heat on their people; they allow each employee to set his or her own performance standards.

Judith M. Bardwick, a psychologist and management consultant, has used another typically government-associated term to describe an equally costly corporate malady: *entitlement*. Entitlement is deeply rooted in many businesses.

Bardwick describes business entitlement programs as "giving people reasonably good jobs without documenting what the company gets in return, resulting in people either not working, or people thinking they are working when, in reality, they are not adding anything of value to the business."

In my consulting practice, I routinely observe entitlement programs. Here are a couple of examples:

THE CHRISTMAS BONUS: Every year around Christmas, each employee receives one month's pay as a Christmas bonus.

THE CHRISTMAS GIFT: Every year around Christmas, each employee receives a turkey or a ham.

COST-OF-LIVING PAY RAISE: Every year, each employee receives a cost-of-living increase.

As a general rule, the word "automatic" should never be used when it comes to any form of employee compensation; employees should always have to achieve specific and measurable criteria to earn either a bonus or a pay raise.

Here are just a few of the remarks I hear from employees:

"It's January 10th and I haven't received my raise yet."

Another is, "I received my Christmas bonus last week and all they gave me this year was a check for a lousy $200."

Or, "Can you believe how cheap my company is, all they gave me this year was a discount coupon to spend at the shopping mall."

How many times have you heard a fellow employee make a statement like, "all they gave us this year was another lousy turkey." Or, "those stupid turkeys get smaller and smaller each year. You'd think they would be ashamed to hand them out."

A willingness to accept mediocre performance is also deeply rooted in the culture of many businesses. Most regions have been blessed with such an excellent economy in recent years that many managers have gotten away with this attitude and still done reasonably well.

When managers allow employees to put in 40 hours while the company receives only about 20 hours of productivity, the bottom line takes it on the chin. Managers cannot continue to allow employees to do things "the old way" or "their way" when their performance is dragging down the overall productivity of the company.

Tolerance perpetuates entitlement. Bardwick says, "Organizations have failed to educate their employees that their work is not just the jobs they perform, but their ability to *add value* through their position in the company."

Value equates to earning capacity by the employee for the business. Neither employees nor management can afford to become complacent by believing they can continue to live off the successes of the past. If they do, the competition is likely to strip them of several of their best customers.

How do you eliminate or prevent the entitlement mindset? Begin by defining individual performance goals and clearly communicating them in measurable terms. Then review results, reward accomplishment, and take swift action with those who refuse to participate in the program.

Performance goals must be measurable. *(See Chapter 1.)* They can be measured daily, weekly, monthly, or via annual standards. How frequently you give measurable feedback depends on the job function, but what is most essential is that you keep score. Otherwise, how can you possibly know the degree to which each employee is contributing?

To make this point, I often ask my audiences sports-related questions. What's the magic batting average that a position player must achieve in baseball to be considered a cut above? The answer is .300. How many RBI must a player achieve in a season to be considered a cut above? The answer is 100. Or how about keeping score among pitchers? How many games must pitchers win to set themselves apart from the pack? The answer is 20.

There are examples from all sports. In football, how many yards must a running back gain in a game, in a season, or on a carry? The answers are 100, 1,000, and 5, respectively.

If I were to tell you that I am an incredibly good golfer, what questions might you ask me to determine my degree of excellence? Your questions might include: What's your handicap? Or, what do you typically shoot?

Back to business. One rule that I have always believed to be important is to provide feedback to all employees on a consistent basis. But the lower an employee's pay range, the more frequently I recommend that managers not only provide feedback, but also reward more positive levels of performance.

The days are long gone when businesses can sit back and wait for their salespeople to pick up the phone. Every salesperson must meet minimum standards both in maintaining product penetration among current customer accounts and in bringing in a budgeted amount of fresh new business.

Operations managers, for example, can no longer allow their personnel to set their own work pace. The individual productivity of each person must be measured and minimum standards established. When an individual employee consistently falls below the minimum performance levels that have been established, that employee must be counseled.

Virtually every company has employees who have made it their life's work to beat the system. The larger the company, the more prevalent this mindset. Too many such entitlement holders eat away at the bottom line and set a costly example within the organization.

If you want to earn a satisfactory level of profit, management must be tough-minded, but fair. When I single out clients who put the most money on the bottom line, they almost invariably set high performance standards for both themselves and the entire organization. They don't put up with mediocrity.

As you begin a new business period—month, quarter, or year—I encourage you to discipline yourself to help your employees be all they can be. Push them. Encourage them. Measure them. Reward them. And remember, if you continue doing the same things year after year that you have always done, you'll most likely get the same results you've always gotten. If you want different results, you must do different things.

MANAGEMENT MISTAKE 20

Failure to Terminate an Employee You've Given Up On

No manager enjoys having to go through the termination process, even when the cause was justified and well-documented. This reluctance, however, can have several disastrous effects.

Effective managers must eventually come to the realization that they are doing unproductive employees no favors when they don't go ahead and ask them to leave.

Just think about it. How would you feel if you learned your boss had given up on you two years ago and was sitting around waiting for you to steal something—or do something equally unacceptable—to make terminating you a slam dunk? It's simply not fair to allow an employee to miss out on an opportunity to find another job in another company where he or she could perhaps excel.

A Test That Answers the Question: To Fire or Not to Fire?

Managers who are straddling the fence on whether to terminate an employee can make a decision by taking this simple test.

Just answer this question: If the employee in question were to walk into your office and tell you that he or she had accepted a position at another company, would you be elated or despondent?

If your answer is, "That would solve about 90% of my business problems," your decision is made.

If your answer is that you would be devastated, then you need to work with the employee to help him or her become more productive.

Holding onto an unproductive employee is horrible for employee morale. It's difficult to motivate your other employees to achieve lofty goals when they see a fellow employee getting away with an unacceptable level of performance. "If Anthony can keep his job with the kind of results he's putting on the board, why should I bust my butt?"

Employees are not stupid; they know when a particular employee is not pulling his or her weight. So managers who don't step up to the plate and do the right thing cannot expect to have the respect of the productive members of their staff.

For an organization to successfully compete in today's marketplace, it needs to field a highly productive team. Any manager who puts up with mediocrity faces the risk of not only losing face with team members, but losing market share to the competition, as well.

Dishonest Employees

Any act of dishonesty or unethical behavior is almost invariably a justifiable reason for termination.

Believe it or not, the rumor spreads rapidly among the company's employees when a fellow employee is stealing from the company. This is true even when the owner or manager is unaware of the dishonest behavior.

So when it is determined beyond the shadow of a doubt that an employee is in any way being dishonest, there is no choice except to dismiss the individual.

Even though this next rule is violated many times by compassionate managers who don't want to go through the hassle of prosecution, I believe a dishonest employee should be prosecuted. Otherwise, the employee will most likely prey upon another business manager, often in your own community.

If you've ever hired an employee who you later learned was terminated from another local business for dishonesty, I believe you'll agree that prosecuting the employee would have been the right thing to do.

MANAGEMENT MISTAKE

Failing to Establish Minimum Conditions of Employment

Most businesses have established *unwritten* conditions of employment, such as a policy against coming to work under the influence of an illegal substance, drinking alcohol or using illegal drugs on company property, testing positive for illegal drugs, initiating violence in the workplace, insubordination, losing one's temper with a customer, etc. Violate one of these rules and most employees will find themselves looking for another job.

It's the less obvious violations, however, that get managers in trouble and reduce organizational productivity.

Conditions of employment should be measurable, or at least clearly observable. They should not be vague or opinion-based. A dress code is an example. If a dress code is implemented, it should be so specific that there is no room for disagreement.

RULE: If there are loopholes in any company rule, employees are certain to find and exploit them.

I compare minimum conditions of employment to professional athletes playing for a professional team. Baseball is a good example. When a position player signs a contract with a baseball team, the team manager explains to the player what is expected of him in *measurable* terms. I expect the following:

- A minimum of a .350 on-base percentage.
- A minimum of 250 runs scored.
- A minimum of 90 runs batted in.
- A minimum of a .950 fielding percentage.
- A minimum of 20 stolen bases.

In the case of a pitcher, the list might read more like the following:

- A maximum earned run average of 3.20.
- A minimum of 15 games won.
- Opposing batters achieve a maximum of a .250 batting average.

These are strictly examples, but they illustrate the point I'm trying to make. And on top of establishing such minimum conditions of employment up front, a professional athlete is often paid a bonus tied to his ability to achieve or exceed minimum standards.

The purpose of written conditions of employment are to make it crystal clear to all employees what they must accomplish in measurable terms to keep their jobs. In the absence of minimum conditions of employment, unnecessary disputes frequently occur between management and their direct reports.

In a business, the minimum conditions will also vary according to the position the employee holds in the company.

The following are the types of minimum conditions of employment that might be made a part of the company's employee manual. Each employee would be required to sign and date the page indicating that it had been read and understood:

- Nothing marked confidential or listed on the following list of confidential information may be removed from company property without written permission from your direct supervisor.
- No company products, office supplies, or tools may be removed from company property without either an invoice or special written permission from your direct supervisor.
- No alcohol or illegal drugs may be consumed on company property.

A **general manager** might be asked to agree to the following conditions of employment to keep his or her job:

- Achieve a minimum return on beginning stockholder's equity of _____%.
- Achieve a minimum return on beginning assets of _____%.
- Control inventory shrinkage to a maximum of __% of sales.

- Put a minimum of ____% of sales on the pretax line.
- Limit capital expenditures not to exceed the agreed-to capital expenditure budget.

A new **road salesperson** might be asked to agree to the following conditions of employment to keep his or her job:

- Bring in a minimum of $____ in new business from new customers.
- Improve customer penetration by ____%, from ____% at the beginning of the year to ____% by December 31.
- Achieve a minimum gross margin of ____%.
- Control sales expenses to not exceed $____ per month, or ____ percent of sales.
- Turn in expense reports for the current month no later than the 5th day of the following month.
- Unless on vacation, attend each local customer association meeting over the course of the year.
- Unless on vacation, attend the monthly sales meeting on the first Monday of each month.

Consider the following conditions of employment for an **inside salesperson** servicing customers:

- Greet each customer with a smile and an offer to be of service.
- Achieve product knowledge goals by scoring a minimum score of ____ on the company's product knowledge quiz.
- Never argue with a customer.

- Treat each customer with a high level of respect as described in the sales manual.
- Help customers choose the product(s) that best fit their individual needs.

The following might be among the conditions of employment that are given to a new **operations manager**:

- Control monthly operating expenses in your area of responsibility to a maximum of ____% of sales.
- See to it that all equipment is serviced according to the published schedule.
- Be accountable for making sure all gates to the warehouse and yard are locked at ____ p.m.
- Control employee turnover in the operations area to a maximum of ____% annually.

The following are among the conditions of employment a **credit manager** might be given:

- Without receiving special permission, average accounts receivable collection days may not exceed ____.
- Credit applications will be turned around in a minimum of ____ hours from time of receipt.
- Each past-due customer will be contacted within ____ days of becoming past-due.
- Bad debt expenses may not exceed ____% of sales.

The following are among the conditions of employment a **buyer** or **purchasing agent** might be given:

- Inventory turnover will be a minimum of ____.

- The inventory fill rate will be no less than _____%.
- The minimum gross margin achieved on the products you purchase will be _____%.
- A minimum of _____ new product lines will be added during the coming year.
- Each new product line will achieve a minimum GMROI of _____.

Depending upon the violation, management should also make it clear—in writing—what the *consequences* will be for failing to achieve the established and agreed-to minimum conditions of employment.

While consequences could include loss of job, they also could include being written up or placed on probation.

MANAGEMENT MISTAKE

Giving the Same Rate of Pay Increase to All Employees

Believe it or not, one of the worst messages a manager can send to the company's employees sometimes comes in the form of their annual pay raise. When all employees receive an identical pay increase—whether it's the same dollar amount or the same percentage increase—management is sending the message that everyone has performed equally well or equally poorly.

RULE #1: All pay raises should be tied to merit. And the best way to determine what an employee's merit raise should be is to make it perfectly clear on what measurable criteria each employee's raise will be based. In other words, what must this employee accomplish in measurable terms to earn a larger-than-average raise in pay?

In my consulting practice, I typically ask the employees I interview this question: what is a typical pay raise that you might expect? In recent years, the typical answer is in the neighborhood of 3% to 4%.

My next question is: what would you have to do to earn double the typical raise that over the years you've come to expect? The typical answer is, "I have no idea." Or, "I don't have a clue." Or, "You tell me, I'd like to know."

This kind of answer is a serious indictment of the professionalism of the company's management team. And on top of that, such a company is missing out on one of its best opportunities to improve organizational productivity, one employee at a time.

I realize that I repeat this statement quite often, but *employees must understand that their raise will not become effective until they do.* This means that the amount of each merit increase should be tied to something measurable that both the employee and his or her manager have agreed upon. It is only via this methodology that money motivated employees can be in control of their economic destiny.

This is one reason that as a salesperson I have always enjoyed being employed in positions that paid me a commission tied to sales and gross margin. Or as a manager, my bonus might be tied to how much money I could put on the bottom line compared to plan. When this has been the case, I never felt that I had been mistreated by management; I knew what I had to do to improve my level of compensation. The sky was the limit. But in reality, my talent and my willingness to work on improving my level of productivity were the only limitations I had to deal with.

So if you wish to make pay raises a motivator, make sure your people understand specifically what they have to do to earn a BIG one.

MANAGEMENT MISTAKE
23

Giving All Employees
a Raise on the Same Day

While my readers may have a valid argument that this practice is not exactly a major mistake, I certainly don't recommend it.

The larger a company or department becomes, the more time-consuming it becomes for managers to conduct performance reviews. During this period of time—often a week or more—managers have time to get little done except conduct performance reviews.

Performance reviews are also a grueling and stressful task—especially in the case of reviews that are not positive. As a result, managers may begin the review process with a positive, patient, and conscientious attitude, but over the course of several days' work, the reviews become more and more monotonous, so much so that the quality of the reviews can deteriorate. So this is one very valid reason not to tie all employee raises to the same period of time on the calendar.

Another reason I disagree with this policy is because employees know when performance reviews are taking place and raises in pay are being given, so productivity in the entire organization is often negatively affected as the grapevine becomes more and more active among personnel.

"Have you received your review yet? How did it go? Did you get a raise? How much did you get?"

Pretty soon, the entire organization is aware of the tone of the reviews and the general amount of each raise.

I recommend that managers consider giving pay raises and conducting performance reviews on each employee's anniversary date. This spreads out the review process and affords management more time and individual attention to each employee they must review.

MANAGEMENT MISTAKE

Failure to Manage the Business "By the Numbers"

Like just about anything in life, better decisions are more often made when managers are able—to the best of their ability—to keep their emotions out of the process. One of the best ways I've found to accomplish this is to manage the business "by the numbers." When I say managing by the numbers, I mean using more objective criteria than emotions as a basis for making decisions. If the numbers a manager is basing his decisions on are accurate, they become an outstanding management tool.

Making the decision to hire one or more new employees is an excellent example. It has been my experience that the impetus for the decision to hire a new employee originates not always with owners and managers, but from within the ranks of the organization. An employee—and frequently multiple employees—will approach the manager with stress written all over her face and explain that the current team is overworked and needs more help.

I heard a counter salesperson in a retail store say once, "We're covered up out here. Sometimes [customers] are four and five deep waiting in line for the next available salesperson. Why yesterday, I even saw several customers drop the items they were intending to purchase on the floor and walk out."

Here's what an operations manager told me he frequently heard from his delivery drivers: "You're killing us out here in this heat. If we don't get some more help, you're going to see a mass resignation. It's not right to work people this hard. We're constantly shorthanded."

If you were a manager without statistics to research, wouldn't you have the tendency to respond to either of these situations by taking some proactive steps to bring on board some additional staff?

While this sort of action seems logical, it may not be logical at all. In the case of the retail salesperson, what if the salespeople on the front counter are averaging 15% fewer transactions this quarter than they averaged this same quarter a year ago? Or in the case of the drivers, what if you did some research and learned that the team of drivers is averaging significantly fewer deliveries year-to-date versus the same period last year? If you had access to these kinds of statistics, you would probably come to the conclusion that organizational productivity was the culprit, not that there was too little "help."

Here's an example of how managing your business by the numbers can help. Many managers find it helpful to maintain records as follows:

- Gross profit per full-time equivalent employee.
- Personnel-related expenses (salaries, group medical insurance, worker's compensation insurance, payroll taxes) as a percentage of gross profit generated during a specific period of time.
- Personnel-related expenses as a percentage of the total operating expenses of the business.
- Sales per payroll dollar.
- Units produced during a given period of time.

Armed with statistics like these, managers are in a better position to determine if the persuasive tactics their employees are using are merely motivated by a desire to reduce the workload or if they are, in fact, overworked. If any of the above measurements show a huge spike in productivity, then perhaps the employees have a point. But if not, perhaps management should resist these requests for more help and spend some additional time working on improving organizational efficiency.

Today's computer systems make it easier than ever to track productivity by job function, work team, department, etc. By graphing these productivity statistics, managers are in a much better position to optimize productivity. *(Also see Chapter 2 on Budgeting.)*

MANAGEMENT MISTAKE

Failure to Benchmark

Management is a difficult job, but as I discussed in the last chapter, it's more difficult when managers fail to manage by the numbers.

The greatest success I have had in my consulting practice can be attributed to establishing benchmarks for success. In the absence of establishing optimal productivity benchmarks, it is extremely difficult for managers to make many of the day-to-day decisions the management position calls for.

During the 35+ years that I have worked with business owners, I have analyzed thousands of financial statements. And when a business is not earning a satisfactory profit on the bottom line, the problem can almost always be traced to too many people in relationship to the gross profit the business is generating. There are certainly other issues that can affect profitability, but in my experience, causes can usually be traced to either the number of people on the payroll or the amount of productivity the employees are generating.

Before I begin a consulting assignment, I ask to see income statements and balance sheets for the current year-to-date and for the previous three years, as well as a list of employees and their job titles.

When working with retail clients, my first calculation is to divide the number of full-time equivalent employees (one 40-hour employee or two 20-hour part-timers would equal one full-time equivalent) into the gross profit dollars the business generates in a 12-month period. The result will tell me the average gross profit dollars generated per full-time equivalent employee. The most accurate way to determine this benchmark is to also take into consideration the number of overtime hours.

Depending on the industry and the gross margin generated by various businesses, the benchmark will vary, but as this number decreases, so does the net profit margin of the business. To remedy this problem, the company must either reduce the number of people in its work force to bring this benchmark in line with industry standards or increase the productivity of its employee base.

A positive way to look at this problem is as untapped capacity. In other words, the company is not operating at its full capacity. If the company could raise sales and consequently the gross profit dollars it generates without having to hire additional personnel, a huge percentage of this additional incremental gross profit would drop directly to the bottom line.

IDEA: Ask each of your key managers how much more sales volume they believe they could process without having to add any new employees. Just as an example, let's assume that their answer is $1 million in additional sales, and your company's gross margin is 25%. This means that by selling the unused capacity of your business, approximately 80% of this fresh $250,000 in incremental gross profit would drop to the bottom line.

Another personnel-related expenses benchmark that is not as dependable, but is nonetheless worthwhile, is to divide personnel-related expenses by total operating expenses. The only negative to this calculation comes when the business's operating expenses are bloated, leaving room for excessive personnel-related expenses.

For this reason, I believe it is more eye-opening to compare key operating expenses to either sales or gross profit.

Here are a few samples of additional benchmarks I have found to be useful:

- Delivered sales per truck.
- Returned merchandise as a percentage of sales.
- Shrinkage as a percentage of sales.
- Bad debt expense as a percentage of sales.
- Percentage of past-due customers in each aging field.
- Sales expense as a percentage of sales and gross profit.
- Average number of lines on all sales tickets written over a given period of time.
- Number of units manufactured in a given period of time.
- Overtime compared to plan.

Ipsative Measurements

If you have no access to benchmarks for your specific industry, I suggest establishing them yourself by comparing your company's best-ever performance to current performance.

By *ipsative* (a psychological term), I mean measuring your company's current level of performance against your company's previous levels of performance rather than against other companies in your industry.

If you have ever watched the Olympic Games on TV or heard commentators cover an athletic event, you'll frequently hear the term "personal best." When a runner runs a race faster than he or she has ever run it before, the runner achieves a *personal best*. When a weight lifter lifts more weight than he has ever lifted in the past, he has achieved a personal best.

Achieving a personal best doesn't necessarily mean that the athlete won the event or even placed, for that matter. It just means that the athlete has never in the past performed that particular event as well as he or she performed it this time.

I believe it's because the athletic world does such an excellent job of keeping a record of athletes' performances each time they compete that each year athletes run faster, jump higher, lift more, and so on.

If you're not keeping score in your business, it's difficult to know whether you're winning or losing; that is, whether you're making progress or losing ground.

Can you imagine how much fun it would be to watch a basketball game if no one kept score? I can't imagine that there would be many players or spectators who would enjoy such an event. Keeping score not only determines winners, it determines what measurable performance leads to victory.

In a basketball game, for example, the statistics determine why one team won and the other team lost. Statistics like:

- Field goal percentage
- Foul shot percentage
- Number of turnovers
- Number of fouls
- Time of possession

It's similar in football:

- Number of yards gained on the ground
- Passing yardage
- Number of turnovers
- Number of yards penalized
- Time of possession

If you want to optimize profitability in your business, you must be willing to keep score; that is, keep good productivity records.

One of the few success stories in the airline industry is Southwest Airways. Southwest, known as a no-frills budget airline, was the first airline to show a profit following 9/11. It has one of the best track records for profitability in the world.

One of the statistics Southwest is most proud of is how fast it turns around its aircraft. You see, according to Southwest, airlines make money when their planes are in the air, not when the pilots and flight attendants are sitting in the crew lounge waiting to board their next flight.

When Southwest pulls up to the jet way, a recordkeeper records the time the plane arrived. According to my research, Southwest is able to—on average—deplane, clean the plane, refuel, reboard the aircraft, and push back in 20 minutes, while carriers like Delta, United, American, etc., typically take more than an hour, on average, to turn their aircraft around.

How about in your business? If you deliver material to your customers, how long does it take your delivery vehicles—on average—to return from a delivery, reload, and leave for another delivery?

How much do your delivery expenses cost your company as a percentage of sales?

How much could you reduce your delivery expenses as a percentage of sales if you could increase your turnaround time?

How does your turnaround time this year compare to your turnaround time last year? This is an example of an ipsative measurement that, if managed and monitored, could allow you to put more dollars on your bottom line.

MANAGEMENT MISTAKE 26

Failure to Use
Proven Marketing Tools

There are four ways to grow a business:

1. Sell more products and services to existing customers.
2. Add new customers.
3. Add new products and services that you do not currently offer.
4. Expand into new markets.

Businesses that don't take the time to prepare a written marketing plan are not in control of their sales destiny. These businesses are dependent upon inflation or the internal growth of the market to generate compounded sales increases.

Sell More Products and Services to Existing Customers

Few companies I work with are aware of the specific product and service categories each of their customers purchase and do not purchase. When this is the case, management cannot possibly prepare a targeted marketing plan to enable them to take a rifle shot at each customer.

This is the best tool I've found for companies that sell to a targeted customer base. As you can see in Figure 6, the company's product categories are listed down the left side of the page, and the company's customers are listed across the bottom of the page. By drawing horizontal and vertical lines, a grid is created. If the company is receiving a particular product line from a particular customer, an "x" is placed in the box. If the customer is purchasing that product or service from a competitor, the block is left blank.

Whoever is managing sales is now in a position to review each salesperson's customer base and work with the salesperson in developing a marketing plan for each customer, for each product category, or perhaps some of both. For example, let's say that from a review of the penetration index, a sales manager learns that a particular salesperson is selling only a few of his customers a particular product category.

The first task is to figure out why this is the case. Is it because the salesperson lacks the product knowledge to give him the confidence necessary to present the product category? Is it because he lacks presentation skills? Is it because the company's fill rate on this particular product category is so poor that customers have sought

FIGURE 6

Penetration Index										
#1 Product Category	X	X		X		X		X	X	
#2 Product Category	X	X			X			X	X	
#3 Product Category		X	X		X		X		X	
#4 Product Category	X	X		X	X	X			X	
#5 Product Category	X	X	X		X		X	X		X
#6 Product Category		X			X				X	X
#7 Product Category	X	X		X		X	X			
#8 Product Category		X	X	X				X	X	
#9 Product Category		X	X				X			X
#10 Product Category		X			X	X	X		X	
	Customer 1	Customer 2	Customer 3	Customer 4	Customer 5	Customer 6	Customer 7	Customer 8	Customer 9	Customer 10

an alternative source of supply? Once the reason has been determined, management is in a position to take corrective action.

If the reason is determined to be poor presentation skills or a lack of product knowledge, training sessions are in order. If the company's service level is lacking, then the level of service must be elevated. The key is to first determine what the obstacles are, then take the appropriate corrective action.

Add New Customers

Unless a company has a strong new business plan in place, the company is not in control of its destiny. Virtually all businesses lose customers for some reason or another over the course of a 12-month period.

Customers sometimes die and as a result the business ceases to exist. Some customers retire with no successors to perpetuate the business. Some customers' credit privileges are suspended, requiring the customer to look elsewhere for the products they need. And sometimes a competitor outsells the salesperson and takes a good customer away.

Any one of these situations can cause a company to lose customers, and that's why it's imperative to have a business plan in place if you want to offset customer losses with new customers.

Here is my recommendation for a successful new business plan:

Make a list of all the qualified businesses in your trade area; that is, companies that purchase the kinds of products that your company sells. You won't be able to initiate an effective business-to-business marketing plan without such a list. The list can be compiled from prospective customers listed in the Yellow Pages or from the Internet. Market research through an organization such as Dun & Bradstreet is another possibility. You might also want to try obtaining a roster from trade organizations prospective customers may belong to.

The next step is to set aside the prospects that are not creditworthy. Don't discard these prospects entirely, because at some point their creditworthiness may improve and they might become qualified prospects.

Once you have a list of a group of qualified prospects, you're in a position to begin initiating marketing tactics.

In-House Mailing List

Don't underestimate the value of an in-house mailing list. It should include not only customers on the books now, but also prospective customers who don't currently do business with your company or perhaps never have. Each mailing to these customers should make a positive impression on the decision-maker. This is why I recommend educational mailings that help the customer do one of three things:

- Make more money.
- Solve their most pressing business problems.
- Help them become more successful, however they measure success.

This type of mailing is often in the form of an educational newsletter. *To make the mailings most effective, the recipient must perceive them to be of value.* I can't emphasize this point strongly enough.

New Business Incentive Programs

Another effective marketing tool is to get the sales force's attention by paying a special incentive when a salesperson is able to secure a new customer. Managers will establish varying criteria for what is necessary for a new customer to qualify for an incentive payment. For example, a new customer may qualify when his purchases reach a predetermined level. Or perhaps it would take only an initial purchase to qualify a new customer. *(See Appendix V on Incentive Plan Rules.)*

Add New Products or Services

Any time a manager can add a new product or service to the company's offering, sales will be positively affected. For example, fast food restaurants that had exclusively sold lunch and dinner items were able to significantly increase sales when they added breakfast items to their menus. Grocery stores added pharmacies and other products previously available only in drugstores. Home improvement stores added garden centers. Many material supply businesses have successfully added installed sales to their service offerings.

Expand Into New Markets

Another way to grow sales is to expand into markets where your company currently has no presence. Virtually all national chains have employed this marketing technique to grow sales. McDonald's began in California and expanded throughout the world. Home Depot began in Georgia and expanded throughout North

America. So, too, can smaller companies grow their sales by adding locations in communities where they previously had no presence.

An effective marketing plan should include all of these opportunities to grow sales. In the absence of a formal marketing plan, marketing decisions are often made willy-nilly. Salespeople may sell what they choose to sell and not necessarily the full product mix that the company wants them to sell. Salespeople may fall into the rut of spending too much time focusing on existing customers to the detriment of prospecting for new customers to expand their customer base. An existing customer may expand into a new market and a knee-jerk decision is made to open a new location in that market to service the existing customer.

Managers who *plan* will enjoy more marketing success than managers who merely work hard.

MANAGEMENT MISTAKE

Failure to Formally Communicate With Employees

In my consulting practice, one of the most frequent management mistakes I observe is the failure of managers to hold formal monthly meetings with each of the people who report directly to them. I recommend that managers sit down with the people who report to them to review the previous month's results and to discuss the individual's progress on assignments that were agreed upon at the previous month's meeting.

To make the meeting even more effective, maintain a notebook on each of your direct reports. The purpose of the notebook is to record the key items that were discussed and agreed upon at each meeting. Of course, if an interim meeting is held, use the notebook to maintain a written record of what took place.

Here's how this management tool might play out:

"Joe, I need you to make a list of each of our competitors and tell me the strengths and weaknesses of each. Is this something you feel comfortable doing?"

"Sure, that won't be a problem. I'll get right on it."

"How about giving me some idea when you believe you can have this project completed?"

"Oh, I don't know. Can I have two weeks to put it together?"

"I'll tell you what . . . I don't want you to drop everything you're doing to complete this project. Do you believe you can get it finished by our scheduled meeting next month? That's four weeks from now. I know you have a lot on your plate right now."

"Sure, that should be a piece of cake. Consider it done."

"Okay, I'm making a note here in your permanent file that you will finish this project by our next meeting on September 19."

"Great, I'll get started right away."

At next month's meeting, the manager will pull out the notebook and begin checking off each of the items he and this particular direct report had agreed to, including the competitive report.

Poor communication will occur if a manager fails to keep good notes on what was agreed to at previous meetings. If the manager tries to maintain such records from memory, it's the beginning of the end. *Good documentation is critical to an effective executive.* This is especially true when managing salespeople. Unless you are able to document your position, manipulative salespeople who possess really good verbal dexterity will frequently be successful at talking themselves out of a tight situation, leaving the manager frustrated.

Some managers will use a single notebook for a couple of years before having to begin a new one. Managers who utilize this effective management tool will have a written record of every meeting with each person who reports directly to them, thereby dramatically reducing the chances of a misunderstanding.

One of my former bosses had another strict rule. He required each of his direct reports to bring a pad of paper to each monthly meeting. He had learned the hard way that the odds were that if the subordinate kept good notes, the subordinate would be more conscientious in living up to his or her commitments, and disagreements were minimized.

The Natural Hedge

Avoid providing your people with a "natural hedge." For example, when top management makes hiring decisions for middle managers, they are providing them with a "natural hedge." In other words, resist giving your middle managers a built-in excuse that allows them to complain that they only have partial accountability.

The same concept holds true for other positions. If a general manager overrules, say, the credit manager on a key credit-extending decision, it is extremely difficult to hold the credit manager accountable for average collection days or bad debt expense. If the credit manager is exercising poor judgment, then perhaps she should be replaced, but continuously second-guessing her decisions gives her a natural hedge in the year-end review.

MANAGEMENT MISTAKE

Failure to Pay
What It Takes
to Attract Top Talent

There's an old saying in business that you can't get a $70,000 employee by hiring two employees earning $35,000 each. While this is true, many managers make the decision every day to refuse to pay what it takes to attract top talent to their business team. When it comes to people, you get what you pay for.

Just like in pricing, water seeks its own level. The market establishes how much you have to pay for personnel with a given set of talents. Managers who violate this rule will forever be playing catch-up as they attempt to compete against higher-quality business teams.

In the early stages of a business, perhaps the founder possesses enough talent to get the business off the ground, but as the business grows, the founder quickly realizes that he must build a management team. The quality of that management team will ultimately equal the quality of the company.

Several years ago, I had a client who operated in rural towns. His retail business was dependent on the relationships his branch managers were able to establish with local contractors. He was the third generation to manage the business. After more than 70 years of dominating their market area, the larger communities surrounding them began to spill over into these rural communities. Large national contractors looking for affordable land bought up hundreds of acres of available land for development, squeezing out the local builders with whom my client had done business for many years.

All of a sudden, seemingly overnight, the market changed. The small-town managers who had strong relationships with the local builders found themselves lacking both the sophistication and the sales skills necessary to penetrate the larger national contractors' organizations. As a result, the market this company once dominated was rapidly being lost to larger competitors that came into their market from nearby cities.

Quality people are an investment intended to provide a substantial return to the company. To receive a high return on your investment in personnel, a manager must make sure that the people he brings on board are highly qualified to do the job at hand.

In my company's recruiting division, we frequently receive calls from clients looking for a manager. After quizzing the caller about the requirements of the job, the next logical question is to ask about the salary the caller has budgeted for the position.

"We'd like to find someone for $45,000, but if we have to go to $50,000, we'll do it."

For $45,000 in today's marketplace, you rarely get a hard-driving, experienced, money-making manager. You can find some terrific human beings who are terrific parents, hard workers, and upstanding citizens who are willing to work for $45,000, but it's almost impossible to find a manager who meets the job specifications who is willing to work for that amount. Why? Because the market has set a substantially higher pay level for a person who can manage a business and give stockholders top dollar as a return on their investment. Owners and managers must be realistic about what they have to pay to attract top talent.

Salespeople are almost always able to set their own earnings level based on how effective they are at making sales. So to attract salespeople who have the raw talent to grow the company's sales, a manager must put together a compensation plan that is competitive in the marketplace. The fortunate thing about salespeople is that they typically are paid on the basis of commission, so their income is in direct proportion to their productivity.

In many organizations, managers are reluctant to allow their salespeople to earn more than key managers. When this is the case, they are never willing to put in place a commission plan that will attract anything more than a journeyman salesperson.

What are journeyman salespeople? These are men and women who already possess product knowledge, so they don't have to be trained in the basics of the products they sell. So in this regard, they can hit the ground running. But what they *don't* possess is aggressiveness, skills of persuasion, and a strong sense of urgency. They are rarely hungry; that is, they are often more interested in pursuing their hobbies than in optimizing their income.

Managers must field a sales force whose combined aspirations are equal to or greater than the aspirations of the manager. When a manager's salespeople are content with only a modest level of income, rarely will the sales of the business soar. Instead, they will merely creep along at about the rate of inflation.

When it comes to hiring people, you get the quality and productivity you're willing to pay for.

MANAGEMENT MISTAKE

Failure to Establish Ethical Standards of Conduct

Any manager living on this planet is aware of the damage that unethical conduct on the part of executive management can do to a company's reputation. There have been several recent examples of such conduct that have made the headlines of financial publications and the front pages of local newspapers (Enron being perhaps the most famous).

When ethical standards are clear within an organization, they begin at the top. Executives who fail to publish such standards and hold all employees accountable for their execution run a high risk that management and non-management personnel alike will make decisions that can lead to irreparable damage to the corporate image.

Frank Bucaro, author of two leading books on ethics (*Taking the High Road: How to Succeed Ethically When Others Are Bending the Rules* and *Trust Me: Insights into Ethical Leadership*), recites the following results from a survey by KPMG, a professional services firm commissioned to survey 2,390 employees:

- 55% of the respondents said their CEO was "unapproachable."
- 61% thought their company would not discipline individuals guilty of an ethical infraction.
- More than 75% had observed violations of the law or of company standards over the previous six months.
- 25% observed company "leaders" withholding information from employees or from the public.

Is it possible that your company could be making decisions that are legal, but unethical? Most executives would answer that this is entirely possible. So ask yourself: How many lawyers do we have on retainer or on our payroll? Then ask: How many ethics advisors do we have on retainer? If the answer is zero for ethics advisors, perhaps your company is vulnerable to ethics violations. (Frank Bucaro is a highly sought-after ethics advisor who consults for corporations. He can be reached via e-mail at frank@frankbucaro.com or by telephone at 800-784-4476.)

Has your company published and posted an "Ethical Code of Conduct"? If not, you should take this initiative immediately. If you don't know where to begin, revisit the Ethics Checklist in Chapter 11.

Ethical Questions for Managers

1. What are the consequences in your company if an employee lies to a customer or supplier?
2. What are the consequences in your company if an employee stretches the truth to a customer or supplier?
3. Do you as an owner or manager set a strong example for ethical conduct?
4. Has your company published a written ethics code of conduct?

(To order books on business ethics by Frank Bucaro, see shopping cart at www.frankbucaro.com.)

MANAGEMENT MISTAKE 30

Hiring Too Quickly,
Firing Too Slowly

Many years ago, I attended a seminar presented by the Chicago-based consulting firm Marketing Personnel Research, Inc., that really opened my eyes to the mistakes I had been making as I stumbled through the hiring process in my own company. After attending that seminar program, my success in hiring improved enormously, so I can personally attest to the value of following the hiring principles I have outlined in this chapter.

Consider this scenario: you will experience the best odds of success if you hire a candidate who possesses 1) the raw talent necessary to perform the job, 2) the appropriate experience; that is, he or she has performed a similar job successfully in the past, and 3) the right chemistry to fit into your organization.

Now ask yourself this question: Which would you eliminate to achieve the second highest odds of success: talent, experience, or chemistry?

Most managers immediately answer experience. The reason: because experience is all that you can teach. Talent and chemistry are pretty much innate. They are very difficult to change.

Yet what is the first thing most managers look for in a candidate? Answer: experience. Am I right? Is this true of the managers in your organization?

SUGGESTION: Hire talent and chemistry first. If a candidate with the right talent and chemistry also has experience, all the better, but resist hiring experience to the detriment of talent and chemistry.

Don't Rush the Hiring Process

Most managers rush the hiring process. The following are a few of the reasons:

1. They have a full-time job that requires 110% of their time. As a result, they recruit and hire in their "spare time."
2. Few managers have had formal training in hiring, so they just do the best they can, often hiring in their own image.
3. They have a position open that is creating a bottleneck, so they are under pressure to fill the job.
4. They don't enjoy the hiring process, so they want to get it over with.

Hire Slowly

My recommendation: Hire slowly. In other words, create a hiring system and slow down the process. A hiring mistake will cost your company many thousands of dollars. In fact, a bad hire may end up costing your company more than if you had left the job open. In reality, managers simply can't afford to make too many bad hires.

Fire Quickly

When it becomes obvious that you've made a bad hire, you live with your mistake far too long in hopes that the candidate's performance will miraculously change. Experience should have taught you, however, that leopards rarely change their spots. In other words, people rarely change their core behavior.

APPENDIX

Position Specification for General Manager, Acme Supply Co.

Acme Supply Co. (ASC) is a successful building material distributor, truss manufacturer, and engineered wood specialist headquartered in Chicago. ASC also operates a truss plant at its main location and a second location in Naperville, Ill., west of the city. This family-owned business projects fiscal next year's sales to be approximately $45 million and is well-positioned to take advantage of the tremendous growth in the Chicago area.

WHY THE POSITION IS OPEN: Owner John Solley has decided to retire within the next few years. ASC has made great strides under Solley's leadership and needs a strong leader to take the company to the next level.

REPORTING: The General Manager will report to John Solley.

SALARY RANGE: A competitive salary plus a performance bonus tied to achieving agreed-to objectives will total well in excess of $100,000. Benefits include a company-matched 401(k) plan (up to 3% maximum), paid vacation, and company car. Reasonable relocation expenses will be reimbursed.

Accountability

1. Achieve realistic budgeted sales and bottom-line objectives for each profit center.
2. Manage and develop all employees to higher levels of productivity and professionalism. Lead a plan of personal development for all ASC personnel.
3. Manage company assets with particular emphasis on accounts receivable and inventory turnover.
4. Maintain and continue to develop the company's strong reputation for quality and service as determined by an annual customer satisfaction survey.
5. Identify and develop new business opportunities to increase profitability. Growth goals have historically been at a 15% compounded rate.

Selecting both the right chemistry and talent for this GM position are equally critical because of the length of time John Solley has led the company. The company's commitment to its employees and customers requires a highly professional GM with excellent people skills. The business also needs a sales-oriented GM who can effectively grow sales while maintaining control of operations. A minimum of five years of successful general management experience in a residential construction-oriented business is required. Experience in managing a business with a truss plant is not mandatory, but would be a nice plus.

Behavioral Requirements

The successful candidate must possess the natural ability to manage; that is, get measurable results with and through others. The individual must be willing to make tough but fair decisions and deal with personnel and customer issues as they arise. There is a friendly, team atmosphere at ASC; an insensitive, hard-nosed management style would be frowned upon. We are looking for a people-oriented manager who will lead the ASC team to achieve the company's long-term goals.

John Solley has been historically committed to providing excellent customer service and quality products. The GM must support this philosophy. The successful candidate must be continuously on the lookout for innovative opportunities to grow the organization.

Because the GM will have a great deal of freedom to manage the organization, this individual must be a self-starter. The successful GM should enjoy working on his own and have the ability to see the big picture while not losing touch with day-to-day operations. The GM should be bright and resilient. Every effort must be made to maximize productivity and efficiency, yet the manager must be able to maintain his focus on long-term goals and objectives.

This person must have the capacity to take ownership of problems and make decisions in critical situations. While a strong work ethic is important, a commitment to results is more important. The successful candidate must possess a track record of managing "by the numbers."

It is important that the individual live up to his commitments to employees, to customers, and to the owner. Strong character and self-confidence are critical ingredients.

John Solley is a very honest and highly committed individual. While these qualities would serve the new manager well, it is equally critical that he possess strong organizational skills. There is a need in this company for more organizational structure.

Administrative skills and the ability to juggle many different responsibilities at the same time are essential to the success of this position.

For more information on this opportunity, or if you wish to recommend a candidate you believe qualifies, please contact (name) at (phone number) and (e-mail address).

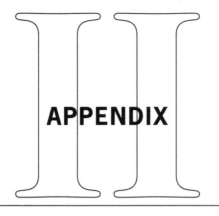

APPENDIX

Recommended Reading List

1001 Ways to Reward Employees, by Bob Nelson.

301 Ways to Have Fun at Work, by Dave Hemsath and Leslie Yerkes.

Blink: The Power of Thinking Without Thinking, by Malcolm Gladwell.

Buy Low Sell High Collect Early and Pay Late, by Dick Levin.

Clean Up Your Act: Effective Ways to Organize Paperwork, by Dianna Booher.

Confronting Reality: Doing What Matters to Get Things Right, by Larry Bossidy and Ram Charan.

Gross Margin: 26 Factors Affecting Your Bottom Line, by Bill Lee.

How to Sell at Higher Prices than Your Competitors, by
   Lawrence L. Steinmetz.
A Life Well Spent, by Russ Crosson.
Moments of Truth, by Jan Carlzon.
The One-Minute Manager, by Kenneth Blanchard and
   Spencer Johnson.
The One-Minute Salesperson, by Spencer Johnson.
The Richest Man in Babylon, by George S. Cason.
*Think and Grow Rich! The Original Version, Restored and
   Revised,* by Napoleon Hill and Ross Cornwell.
Tough Management, by Chuck Martin.
Why Employees Don't Do What They're Supposed to Do,
   by Ferdinand F. Fournies.
You Can Get Anything You Want, by Roger Dawson.

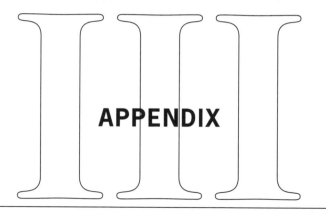

APPENDIX III

Samples of Open-Ended Interview Questions

Management Version

1. Describe your work history, beginning with your first position after you left school. Please elaborate on why you changed either companies or positions.

2. Describe a recent day in your current position, beginning with the time you arrived at work and the time you left for the day.

3. How many hours do you typically work in a week?

4. Describe three of your proudest accomplishments in the past few years.
5. What special talents do you believe you have that will be most valuable to the organization you work for?
6. Please describe yourself using three adjectives.
7. Describe the ideal relationship you would envision having with your manager.
8. How do you typically go about selling your point of view?
9. What would attract you to an opportunity at another organization?
10. Describe a person(s) who has had a strong influence on your adult life. What was the nature of their influence?
11. Who would you say is the most effective manager you ever worked for? Could you describe what made him/her so effective?
12. How would you compare yourself to this person? If we could ask this person to compare himself/herself to you, what do you envision that he/she would say are the primary differences in your respective styles?
13. Who is the least effective manager you've ever worked for? What made him/her so ineffective?
14. When it comes to bosses or supervisors, what are your pet peeves? What are the little things a boss might do that would drive you up the wall?
15. What techniques or methods have you used to ensure that you clearly understand the expectations of your current manager?

16. What methods have you used to ensure that your communication is clearly understood by your employees?

17. What do you especially enjoy about your current (or most recent) job function?

18. How many people would you estimate you have directly hired over the years?

19. What techniques have you found to be most effective to avoid hiring mistakes?

20. What would you say has been your biggest hiring mistake? What did you learn from that experience?

21. When you realize you have an employee you've given up on, what procedure do you typically follow to terminate him/her?

22. Can you think of a recent crisis and describe how you handled it?

23. What methods do you use to measure employee performance?

24. What kinds of employee behaviors really irritate you? How do you communicate this to your employees?

25. What *valid* criticisms have been made of your management style, valid being the key word in this question?

Sales Version

1. Please describe your work history (beginning with your education).

2. Describe your day-to-day activities in either your current or your most recent sales position. What would be a typical day for you?
3. What has been your proudest achievement in professional sales?
4. Looking at your most recent company, what would you do differently if you had the opportunity to begin again?
5. If you were to accept the position we are interviewing you for, how would you envision spending your first 60 days on the job?
6. What level of sales would you envision producing in your first four or five months on the job?
7. What techniques have you found most effective to set your company's products and services apart from your competition?
8. If you were asked to describe yourself using three adjectives, what would they be?
9. How many hours in a week do you expect to work? Or, how many hours in a week are you currently working?
10. Who has had the greatest influence on your adult personality? How would you describe this person's influence? [If necessary, ask the candidate from a professional standpoint.]
11. If you could improve anything about the way your current manager goes about his/her work, what would it be? [If necessary, ask about the most recent manager if the person is unemployed or between jobs.]
12. Who was the best manager you've ever worked for? What made him/her the best?

13. Can you estimate for me what you believe to be a reasonable dollar volume of sales for a salesperson to produce in the position we are interviewing you for?

14. Who was the worst manager you've ever worked for? What made him/her the worst?

15. Who is the best salesperson you've ever worked with? What made him/her the best?

16. How would you compare yourself to this person?

17. If given the opportunity to speak to several of your peers in professional sales, how would they describe your approach to selling?

18. What do you really enjoy about your work? What do you enjoy least?

19. What would you like to be doing five years from now? [If appropriate, ask what steps the candidate is taking to be in this position.]

20. If you were to work with a company for a number of years and then retire, what would you want people to say about you at a going-away party?

21. Please describe your pet peeves; that is, things that really irritate you about others. [If appropriate, emphasize the work environment after he/she gives initial answers.]

22. What has been your proudest achievement as an adult? [If appropriate, ask about professional achievements.]

23. What has been your biggest disappointment as an adult? [If appropriate, ask about professional disappointments.]

24. If you could have done anything differently to have affected this disappointment, what would you have done?
25. If we were to speak to the best manager you've ever worked for, what would he/she say would be the area you need most improvement in?
26. If we were to speak to your current manager [if a different person from above question], what would he or she say would be the area you need the most improvement in?
27. If we were to speak to a number of your customers, what kind of relationship would they say they had with you?
28. If we were to speak to your largest customer, what would he/she say would be the area in which you need the most improvement?
29. Can you describe some of the specific steps you have taken over the years to enhance your professionalism as a salesperson?
30. What is the single, most significant business lesson you have learned in the last year?
31. If you could change or improve one thing about yourself, what would it be?
32. If you were giving advice to a person who was about to enter the world of professional sales in your particular area, what would you tell this person to help him/her be the most successful?
33. What system or technique do you use to organize your time?
34. Do you feel listening skills are an important part of selling?

    A. How would you describe your listening
       skills?

    B. What steps do you feel you could take to
       improve your listening skills?

35. Can you provide several specific examples of things you have done that represent outstanding customer service?

36. What *valid* criticism, if any, has been made regarding your sales style, valid being the key word in this question?

37. What are your hobbies and personal interests?

38. Based on your understanding of the position thus far, what would need to occur for you to want to join this organization?

39. Why should we choose you for this opportunity?

40. Is there anything else you wanted to tell us about yourself that we didn't ask?

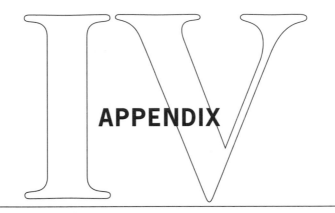

Position Specification Questionnaire

The purpose of the position specification process is to guide a manager or a team through a thought process that will produce a behavioral position specification; that is, a clear picture that will enable all concerned to envision the behavioral characteristics the ideal person for the job will possess.

The position specification can be used as a:

- *Scorecard*: To evaluate applicants for the position.
- *Benchmark*: For a manager to assess existing employees in a specific position.

In addition to producing a behavioral profile, this exercise also provides:

- A road map for a new employee to follow for the first few months on the job.
- Management training for those involved in the development of the profile. This process will assist managers to be better decision-makers in the most critical decisions they will ever make: whether to hire, retain, promote, or terminate.

The process involves three steps:

1. **Information Gathering:** Gathering input from the individual manager or a team regarding the behaviors required to get the job done.
2. **Identification of Behavioral Characteristics:** Determining the behavioral characteristics that are required to be successful in a particular position.
3. **Prioritization of Characteristics:** Deciding which of the behavioral characteristics are the most critical for success in the job.

If a team approach is used to prepare the position specification, the group should be composed of four or five individuals who really understand the position or are insightful enough to provide relevant input. Generally, the person to whom the position will report should serve as team leader. The manager should make the final decision since it is the manager who must be accountable for the results of his or her team members.

Position Specification Interview Guide

A. Basic information
- Position
- Supervisor

- Key peers
- Direct reports
- Number of people in this work unit
- Overview of responsibilities:

Additional information for sales positions
- Territory
- New or existing territory?
- Overnight travel required?
- Types of products or services
- Types of accounts
- Measurable goals
- Prospecting information (percent of time, percent goal)
- Service to existing customers (percent of time, percent goal)
- Describe any unique or special personal qualities necessary to successfully sell these particular products or services.

B. Previous history with this position
- Why is this position open?
- If this is a replacement:
  1. What were the positive characteristics of the former job holder? (What are you going to miss most about not having him or her in the position?)
  2. If anything, what characteristics of the former job holder do you wish to avoid duplicating when selecting his or her replacement?
  3. Are there any other people in your organization who can perform one or more of the job functions? If so, who?

4. Is it at all possible this position can be eliminated?

C. Primary activities (be specific and break down the activities into daily, weekly, and monthly; include the percent of time spent on each activity and the characteristics required)

D. What specific accomplishments are expected in the first 3 months? What tangible evidence will you look for to make sure you did not make a hiring mistake?

E. What specific accomplishments do you expect in 6 to 9 months? What evidence will you look for at this point to be sure you've hired the right person for the job?

F. Education and experience (be realistic and break down the list into required and desired elements)

G. Chemistry
   • Describe the company culture
   • Describe the growth stage of company
   • Explain any recent events affecting position
   • Describe the personality of this particular work team
   • List the manager's pet peeves

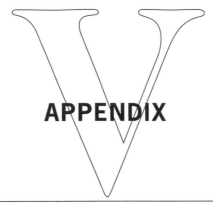

APPENDIX

Rules for
Incentive Compensation

Just about every day, I receive calls from clients interested in installing an incentive plan in an attempt to enhance employee productivity. Since there continues to be a great deal of interest in incentive plans, here are a few of the key rules I have developed over the years:

Rule #1: Nothing is simple.

It's not easy to put together an incentive plan that is fair and that will enhance employee motivation to perform over and above the minimum required to keep his or her job. So if you do decide to install an incentive plan, make sure you think it through.

Rule #2: Decide what results you want before you write the plan.

If you want lower average collection days, higher inventory turnover, lower operating expenses as a percentage of sales, higher gross margins, etc., make sure that the plan is written to reward those behaviors. However, be realistic. Don't make the objectives of the plan so difficult that no one can possibly achieve them.

Rule #3: Put your incentive plan in writing and sleep on it before introducing it to your employees.

If there is a loophole in your plan, your employees will find it.

It's quite easy to overlook the obvious when putting an incentive plan together. That's why it should be put in writing. Read it and reread it. It's even a good idea to ask a trusted employee to read it from an employee's perspective. If there's a flaw in the plan, it's less embarrassing to find the flaw before the plan has been announced.

Rule #4: Explain up front that the plan will be reviewed over the first 90 days and that management reserves the right to tweak the plan if it turns out that anything about it is unfair to either the employees or the company.

Don't fall into the trap of being stuck with a plan that's flawed.

Rule #5: After the plan is announced, organize a series of employee meetings to brainstorm techniques to optimize the results; that is, to achieve the goals the plan rewards.

It's important that this plan be successful. The plan should do the job it's intended to do. If, for example, you're setting up an incentive plan that rewards employees for improving gross margin, hold a brainstorming session to discuss specifically what employees can do to accomplish that result. For example, suggest that they read my book, *Gross Margin: 26 Factors Affecting Your Bottom Line* (www.mygrossmargin.com) and discuss each of the 26 factors individually.

Rule #6: Pay incentive payments in a separate check.

Incentive pay is entirely different from regular pay, so don't intermingle the two in the same paycheck. Should you make the decision to discontinue the plan, you don't want your employees (or their spouses) to perceive that they have received a cut in pay.

Rule #7: Periodically discontinue incentive plans even if they are performing well.

Even eating ice cream becomes old hat if you eat it constantly. To avoid allowing the incentive plan to be taken for granted, suspend it occasionally. During the suspension period, it's a good idea to evaluate the success of the plan and implement any changes that may make the plan more effective when it is reinstated.

Rule #8: Be innovative.

Incentive plans don't have to be restricted to money. Incentives involving dinner for two, a luxury hotel room for the weekend with room service, a delivery of Omaha Steaks, travel, premiums, a day off with pay, etc., can be just as effective. When deciding what to offer as an incentive, make sure the reward is commensurate with the accomplishment.

For example, a $100 bill won't inspire an employee who earns, say, $50,000 a year as much as it will an employee who earns, say, $20,000 a year. It's important that the incentive you offer is significant enough to alter the employee's lifestyle.

While your more highly compensated employees might turn up their nose at a $100 bill, a gift certificate worth $100 at a prestigious restaurant that they might not otherwise patronize could be attractive to this same group of employees. It's not always how much you spend, but how you spend it.

And don't discount the value of plaques, a framed letter of commendation from the president of the company, or another form of award the employee can display.

Individual goals are effective, but so are team goals. You might offer an incentive to an inside salesperson who is able to generate one additional point of gross margin in a given month. You might also offer an award to the entire inside sales team if, as a group, they are able to reduce one-line sales tickets to a specified level.

Here are some incentive plans that have worked well for others:

- Reward an outside salesperson for bringing in a new customer who places an initial order worth a specified amount of money.
- Pay a higher commission on emphasis product lines.
- Pay drivers an incentive for increasing their average number of stops or deliveries.
- Pay an incentive to the entire operations team for reducing the average turnaround time for getting delivery vehicles back out on the road after returning from trips.
- Pay an incentive to loaders or order-pullers for each ticket they fill.
- Pay an incentive to buyers for increasing inventory turnover or for reducing shrinkage.
- Pay an incentive to credit managers for reducing average collection days or for reducing bad debt expense.
- Pay an incentive to production workers for improving production.

Rule #9: Incentive plans are no substitute for management.

Managers cannot rely on incentive plans to do their jobs for them; they still have to manage.

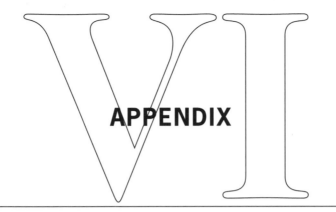

APPENDIX VI

Strategic Planning Questionnaire

There are many processes that companies use to arrive at a strategic plan, and answering strategic questions is one of them. I've put together several key questions that your strategic planning committee should answer. The answers to these strategic questions and to the discussion questions I have included, as well, will give you the information you need to hammer out a strategic plan for your company.

The ultimate questions the strategic plan must answer are:

1. Where are we going? What is our management team committed to accomplish in measurable terms, and over what time frame?
2. How are we going to get there?

3. What obstacles are we likely to face along the way?
    And how will we get around them?
4. What is our action plan? What will we do differently to achieve more effective results?

It's better to answer question #1 in terms of the compounded earnings growth rate your management team wishes to commit to rather than planning a specific long-term sales goal. Hypothetically, you might agree to grow the company at an average compounded rate of earnings growth of, say, 20%. What I like most about an *average* compounded rate of earnings goal is that it allows for years when the housing economy is not as strong as others.

Rule of 72

By dividing the compounded rate of growth your strategic planning team agrees on into 72, you will determine the number of years it will take your company's sales to double. If you were to select a 15% compounded rate to grow your company, sales will double in 4.8 years.

QUESTION #1: What rate of compounded earnings growth do you wish to commit to? (In later exercises, I'm using 20% . . . strictly as an example.)

DISCUSSION QUESTIONS: Is each member of our team willing to make the personal commitment to achieve the above growth goal? What personal sacrifices will each of us be required to make that perhaps we are not making now?

QUESTION #2: Do we have the resources to achieve the above growth goal?

DISCUSSION QUESTIONS: Discuss *each resource* that's required (e.g., capital, each location's physical facilities, management and sales acumen).

If, for example, your team were to commit to a 20% compounded earnings growth goal, your company would likely double in sales in 3.6 years. In 7.2 years, your company's sales would quadruple.

QUESTION #3: If you do not have sufficient capital or if you are not earning sufficient capital to support a 20% compounded growth rate, where would the capital come from?

QUESTION #4: What is the capacity of each of your existing locations? At what sales level do you anticipate that each of your existing facilities would reach capacity?

DISCUSSION QUESTIONS: Which locations can be expanded to increase capacity? Which locations cannot be expanded (e.g., locations that are landlocked)?

QUESTION #5: Do your existing key personnel possess the talent, skills, tenacity, and experience to manage a business that will double and then quadruple its current size?

DISCUSSION QUESTIONS: Review with each manager and each member of the top management team individually, and make an attempt to determine (in your collective opinions) which individuals can definitely rise to the occasion and which individuals will begin to lose altitude at double and quadruple their current levels of responsibility and accountability.

DISCUSSION QUESTIONS: What specific additional training would each individual require to enable each to operate successfully at double and quadruple their existing level of responsibility? Which individuals do you believe will "max out" at these sales levels regardless of the amount of additional training they receive?

QUESTION #6: What products might you be manufacturing or selling in the future that you do not sell today?

How will the additions of these products affect your physical facilities and your personnel?

QUESTION #7: What future markets will your company be operating in that you do not operate in today? What logistical factors need to be taken into consideration?

QUESTION #8: How do you anticipate that your customer base will change over the next five to eight years? How will these changes affect your company? What must you do differently to accommodate these changes?

QUESTION #9: How do you believe your operating expenses as a percentage of sales compare to each of your key competitors in each of the markets you serve? Are your operating expenses as a percentage of sales a *strength* or a *weakness* as you strive for your compounded earnings growth goal?

QUESTION #10: How do you believe that your current strategic marketing plan must be modified to generate the additional sales to accommodate a 20% compounded growth goal?

Critical internal review of your company

- What are your strengths? By location, in what specific areas do you outshine the competition?
- What are your internal weaknesses? By location, in what areas do your competitors outshine you?
- How do your customers and prospects perceive your company? What is your reputation in each of the markets you serve?
- If your customers have complaints about your company, what do you suppose they are? Answer by individual location.

External review of local conditions

- What changes are taking place in each market you serve that could impact your company? How fast is each market projected to grow, in terms of housing forecasts, demographic projections, and so on?
- Most important, how does your company stack up in the local business environment in each of the markets you serve? (Assess how you rank by key criteria; i.e., equipment, physical facilities, quality of sales personnel, product offerings, terms of sale, etc. Add other criteria you believe are key.)
- What's your market share in each market you serve? (If, for example, your company were to have, say, 65-70% market share in a particular market, odds are not good that that amount of market share can be improved.)
- What's your relevant market share? Estimate what percentage of your existing customers' total purchases are purchased from your company in each market you serve. (The answer to this question will help determine the extent to which your company must bring in new customers to achieve the company's growth goals. Or can you do so by increasing your relevant market share with existing customers?)
- **Key success factors:** Brainstorm and name all of the keys to success in your business and how you believe your customers would say you stack up compared to *each* of your key competitors—by location. (This may be a good exercise for smaller breakout groups.)

Examples:

- What specific services do you perform that are key to your success? List as many as possible. Look at each individual service and determine how you rank by location. What factors are preventing you from ranking #1 in each location?
- How about the quality of the products you supply?
- Depth and breath of inventory.
- Your capital position.
- Your credit policy.
- The competitiveness of your prices.
- Your delivery equipment.
- Your physical facilities.
- Your customer contact personnel.

RECOMMENDATION: It's often easy for a group of managers to allow the discussion to go off on tangents and fail to stick to strategic issues. This is where a strong facilitator comes in. Someone must play the role of facilitator and be politely forceful enough to keep everyone on task.

Sometimes you can make faster progress if you divide these questions among smaller groups and regroup after a predetermined period of time to share the results of your discussions. If you do decide to take this approach, each small group will need to select a facilitator to keep discussions on track.

I also recommend that your strategic planning committee go off-site for this process so you will be less distracted by noise from office telephones and pagers.

Order More Copies of this Book

To get additional copies of this book, please contact us with the following information.

- Number of copies—$21.95 per copy plus $6.50 shipping in the U.S. and Canada, US$10 shipping outside North America
- Name
- Company
- Address
- City, state and zip
- Telephone number
- E-mail
- Method of payment—send a check or provide a Visa, MasterCard, AMEX, or Discover number and expiration date and your signature

If you would like to receive Bill Lee's electronic newsletter or would like more information on seminar programs by Bill Lee, please contact us.

Contact information
Telephone: 1-800-476-8722, ext. 42376
Fax: 509-267-9711
Mail: 30 Ways, P.O. Box 5558, Greenville, SC 29606.
E-mail: to blee@BillLeeOnLine.com
Web site: www.BillLeeOnLine.com

This book is available at special quantity discounts to use as premiums and sales promotions, or for use in corporate training programs. For more information, please call the Special Sales Manager at 800-476-8722, ext. 42369, or write to New Oxford Publishing of North America, P.O. Box 5558, Greenville, SC 29606.